HE MARRIED A SOCIOPATH

HE MARRIED A SOCIOPATH

A Navy SEAL Team VI Sniper's Greatest Threat Lived in His Own Home

DR. SABRINA BROWN

ERUDITE PRESS

Copyright © 2019 by Sabrina Brown DrPH

All rights reserved.

No part of this book may be reproduced in any form or by any electronic or mechanical means, including information storage and retrieval systems, without written permission from the author, except for the use of brief quotations in a book review.

ISBN: 978-1-937979-72-0

Erudite Press

Goshen, Kentucky 40026

www.eruditepress.com

Dedication

This book is dedicated to my parents, and to the memory of Steven's grandparents, Jack and Lee, for their unconditional love and support. I also dedicate this book to my precious son, who suffered abuse at the hands of a male and female sociopath.

Untitled

"When a parent teaches their child to hate then their love for the child becomes second to the hate. Like love can do, hate conquers all. It wipes out goodness and light. Our family will be a family of love; to be a part of this family means to love every member. Hate will not live in our home." ~Sabrina

DISCLAIMER: All names of family and friends have been changed to respect their privacy.

Foreword

It is such a joy for me to work with authors, and to help shape their narrative into a publishable book, always mindful of each individual's unique writing style and voice. This is certainly true with Dr. Sabrina Brown's second book titled *He Married A Sociopath: A Navy SEAL Team VI Sniper's Greatest Threat Lived in His Own Home*.

Dr. Sabrina Brown is an Associate Professor, in the Department of Epidemiology, College of Public Health, at the University of Kentucky. Her primary research interests have focused on violence prevention, including intimate partner violence. Knowing just a little bit about her background before I began editing this book, my preconceived expectation was that I would be reading a clinical manuscript, perhaps heavy on personal research. What I didn't expect, however, was a deeply personal and heart-wrenching story about her husband (a highly decorated U.S. Navy SEAL) and Dr. Brown and the verbal, psychological and financial abuse they both suffered in their first marriages. As the story unfolds, I began to more fully understand what it means to be in the emotional grasp of a sociopath—and the terror—the on-going emotion assault—and the damage—that a sociopath can wreak on the lives of others.

Dr. Brown expertly intertwines their personal stories with in-depth professional research to describe Parent Alienation Syndrome and how very challenging (how exhausting) it is to fight every day on the domestic battlefield for parental freedom, and to be an active part of their child's life. She further delves into the research many psychologists have documented on dysfunctional divorce-related syndromes, like The Medea Syndrome and Divorce Related Malicious Mother Syndrome.

I am so appreciative of Dr. Brown for finding her voice and having the courage to write about, and share with others, Steven's harrowing story, and for providing another chapter of her own traumatic story with this follow up to her first self-published book, *I Married A Sociopath: Taken to the Edge of Insanity, My Survival Unexpected*. Through this difficult emotional portrayal of abuse, Dr. Brown educates the reader to more clearly recognize and understand sociopathic behavior, and provide the tools of knowledge to help fight and to not give up when in a similar abusive situation.

Blessings for emotional healing and much deserved love to Dr. Brown and to you, the reader.

Karin Acree

Editor, and Publisher of Derek Publications

Preface

Every story is evidence that someone else is out there.
  ~Daniel Taylor, The Healing Power of Stories

Growing up I endured enough adverse childhood experiences—known as ACEs—that I approached puberty with an unstable and insecure sense of myself, and a distorted perception of my role in relationships. I had been conditioned to devalue my needs and give without question.

I thought I had met the man of my dreams at fifteen, Peter Walton, but by nineteen—pregnant and married—my hopes and dreams of love and romance were crushed. I found myself in a web of violence and psychological games, constantly threatened that if I told anyone or tried to leave, I would lose my children, public respect—everything; it would be easy because I was "crazy."

When I finally began to stand up for myself and asked for a divorce, I found myself in a courtroom being served a thirty-five-page motion and an Emergency Protective Order "protecting" my abuser and children from me. My worst fears and decades of threats had become my reality. My experience during divorce proceedings

Preface

was unjust, I was re-traumatized and helpless. I endured a lifetime of abuse all over again—this time publicly.

I have studied the etiology of violence for almost two decades. My primary research interests are focused on intimate partner violence, suicide, veteran suicide, homicide followed by suicide, nonfatal suicide-related outcomes, infant and child death, elder maltreatment, perpetration of fatal violence, developing statewide surveillance and reporting systems, and system evaluation.

Over the years, as I presented my research and listened to advocates, I realized that my own relationship was fraught with intimate partner problems. I didn't realize that it was violent until I was sitting in that courtroom and advocates explained to me how violent it was. I had recognized that my ex-husband was abusive and a narcissist, but when I finally started the process of separation and leaving, I realized that he was much more: I was dealing with a sociopath. In February of 2012, as the abuse continued following our formal divorce, I started to blog. I took my journaling online, making my story available to others, but under the protection of an alias. I self-published *I Married a Sociopath: Taken to the Edge of Insanity, My Survival Unexpected. This is my Story*, in 2017. The process from blog to book, under my real identity, was agonizingly difficult—an unexpected internal struggle. It took five years to not only write my book, but also to find the courage to uncover and claim myself. Fear got in the way of so much and it kept me imprisoned. My transformation to living freely has manifested, in part, with the publication of my book and writing the rest of my story in this second book; this time with the validation of a publishing house.

Introduction

I take business trips, at least once a year, as part of my job requirements. In May 2010, while on such a trip, I met Steven who was visiting the same city for the same reason. Steven was in the throws of a high-conflict divorce; I was trying to get Peter to leave the house and, ultimately, to obtain a divorce. We not only acknowledged our instant chemistry, we also bonded over shared experiences with our soon-to-be ex-spouses. Even though we lived four thousand miles apart, me in Kentucky and him in Alaska, our chemistry was so intense that we sensed, somehow, we would be together. We saw each other about every three months during our first year together. We were both all-in, but wouldn't cling if it fizzled. We weren't forcing it; if it was meant to be, it would all work out.

Any time something bad happened, my first thought was to tell Steven and his first thoughts were of me. We went back and forth, helping each other defend ourselves against a legal labyrinth of accusations from our spouses who were so similar, it felt like they were reading from the same playbook.

Introduction

Steven and I eloped on June 21, 2013. My son Junior, then nine years old, and I moved to Virginia Beach and into a home with Steven. September 2013 through September 2014 was the worst year that either Steven or I would experience. Peter and Jo (Steven's ex-wife) weren't done with us; they launched a campaign that succeeded in damaging us psychologically, mentally, spiritually and financially. They would not, could not, leave us alone. We had dared to divorce sociopaths…The worst was yet to come…This is OUR story.

ONE

The American War Hero

MAY 21, 2006

He thought about his tombstone—how it would look—him dying on the same day he was born—35 years later. As he waited to jump out of the helicopter, he thought this must be what it felt like landing on the beach at Normandy. Then he took those thoughts, all fear and self-doubt, set them aside and looked down: there was no place for them here.

This was an impossible mission. He was first out heading into darkness facing hundreds against him—only a dozen behind him. The dust from the helicopter and close air support made their usual night vision useless. So Steven, a sniper and point man, put on newly developed night vision/thermal equipment, not yet fully tested and not completely familiar to him. Not only were they going into the heart of enemy territory, in the pitch black, he had to guide the rest of the team's maneuvers and be their eyes as well. Steven led the team through the four-hour gunfight all the while protecting them as a sniper. All of his men survived. The heroic story reads directly from his Silver Star Award as:

> CHIEF OF NAVAL OPERATIONS
>
> The President of the United States takes pleasure in presenting the SILVER STAR MEDAL to:
>
> BOATSWAIN's MATE FIRST CLASS (SEA, AIR AND LAND)
> STEVEN J. BROWN
> UNITED STATES NAVY
>
> For service as set forth in the following
>
> CITATION:
> For conspicuous gallantry and intrepidity in action against the enemy while serving as Reconnaissance Team Leader assigned to a Joint Task Force conducting Special Operations in support of Operation ENDURING FREEDOM on 21 May 2006. Chief Brown led his team in the execution of a daring and complex direct-action assault against a numerically superior and heavily armed enemy. Penetrating enemy territory, his assault force eliminated enemy fighters during a four-hour firefight. Chief Brown repeatedly maneuvered to unsupported and exposed positions to provide cover fire for his assault force. With total disregard for his own safety, he continuously moved toward the enemy, engaging and eliminating three enemy fighters who were attempting to flank his element. Chief Brown's dedication to accomplish the mission and protect his assault team clearly saved their lives. His heroic bravery during intense combat operations was an inspiration to all with whom he served, by his bold leadership, exceptional professionalism, and total devotion to duty, Chief Brown reflected great credit upon himself and upheld the highest traditions of the United States Naval Services.
>
> For the President,
> Admiral, United States Navy
> Chief of Naval Operations

Though earning the Silver Star this was not the most dangerous operation that Steven led; it just happens to be the one that was noticed. The most dangerous operation will be detailed later, by Steven himself.

Steven Brown is now a retired Navy SEAL, who served from May 1994 until June 2014, when he retired as a Senior Chief. Steven was assigned to four SEAL commands during his career, most significantly SEAL Team VI from 2001-2009. While at SEAL Team VI, he served as a point man, assaulter, breacher and sniper. He participated in more than 250 combat operations resulting in being awarded the Silver Star, the third highest award for Valor in Combat; three Bronze Stars, the forth highest award for Valor in Combat; and numerous other personal awards: two Joint Service Commendation Medals, Navy Commendation Medal with combat V for Valor, Joint Service Achievement Medal, two Navy Achievement Medals, three Combat Action Ribbons, Presidential Unit Citation, five Good Conduct Medals, two National Defense Service Medals, three Armed Forces Expeditionary Medals, Afghanistan Campaign Medal with 2 stars, Iraq Campaign Medal with 2 stars, Global War on Terrorism Expeditionary Medal, Global War on Terrorism Service Medal, Armed Forces Service Medal, nine Sea Service Deployment Ribbons, United Nations Medal, Expert Rifleman Medal, Expert Pistol Medal.

Following his years of combat service, Steven served as the Senior Enlisted Advisor of the Sniper Cell developing cutting-edge equipment and providing advanced training for command snipers. After Team VI, Steven was assigned to Naval Special Warfare Basic Training Command Detachment Kodiak, located in Kodiak Alaska as the Senior Enlisted Advisor. While in Alaska, he trained more than 2000 SEALs and other Special Operations Operators in Cold Weather Maritime operations, mountaineering, primitive living, land navigation and modernized equipment and clothing used by SEALs in this environment.

TWO

The Story Behind the American War Hero

Steven grew up in a small beach town in southwestern Michigan. He was born in Germany while his dad was stationed there with the U.S. Army. He and his parents moved to Michigan, where he lived most of his life, when he was just over a year old. His parents divorced when he was in fourth grade, a traumatic event as none of his friend's parents were divorcing and both sets of his grandparents were still married. Divorce was completely new to him. He remembers his parents bringing him and his younger brother, Ross, into the living room and telling them they were divorcing; then there was a knock at the door, it was for Steven. His best friend Billy had come to ask him to play, but Steven was in tears and relayed to his friend the news. He had to leave his friends, his school and his community to move into an apartment—his overall way of life changed drastically.

He lived with his mom most of the time and had visitation with his dad every other weekend. Time with Steven's dad included riding dirt bikes at his great uncle's gravel pit, fishing and other traditionally male activities. Time at Steven's mom's house was different. Steven's mom taught him how to drive a stick shift the summer after the divorce. She told him that she needed him to learn so that he could drive her if she was tired. Steven's mom had him drive part way to his grandparent's house, on active roads, when he was eleven. Steven, during one of his mother's parties, walked into his basement bedroom to find a couple having sex on his bed, another traumatic event. Steven's mom generally used corporal punishment. This escalated to using leather belts; on one occasion, Steven was hit with the metal part of the belt. When, as an adult, Steven confronted his mother about this, her response was that it was not her fault, that the belt had slipped, which made no logical sense to Steven.

The summer after Steven's sixth grade year, the court gave him an option, so he moved in with his dad. He had been intentionally acting out with his mom so that she would want him to leave. Steven and Ross "walked to school" but really hung out at the creek down the street until his mom left for work. Then they went back home for the rest of the day. This went on for weeks until the school contacted Steven's mom to alert her that her sons had been truant. Shortly afterwards, visitation reversed for Steven: his mom got every other weekend. Ross stayed primarily with their mom. Unfortunately, because the boys were separated and were not close growing up, they developed very different perspectives about their upbringing.

Summers, when Steven lived mostly with his mom, he and his brother spent the majority of her allotted time with his maternal grandparents. His maternal grandfather served in the Army, World War II, in the European Theatre. Steven has great memories of his maternal grandfather and extended family members (especially a favorite uncle and aunt) going fishing, ball bearing (BB) guns, pulling weeds in the garden, drive-in movies with aunts and uncles, being a bat boy for his uncle's softball team, riding with his uncle in dump trucks, front end loaders and other heavy equipment, horses, pig farms, chickens, dogs; overall, it was a great place to spend summer vacations. Steven was the first grandchild, and the only for many years, so during those years he had their undivided attention. He has great memories about being with not only his grandfather but also his maternal grandmother. She was loving, attentive, caregiving, nurturing—grandmotherly. He remembers macaroni and tomatoes; something Steven can't stand now, but back then they were top cuisine.

Steven's paternal grandfather also served in the Navy and was in combat in World War II in the Pacific Theatre. Following his military career, he was an entrepreneur; his grandfather took him to work and they traveled together. Steven's dad was an only child and Steven and his brother the only grandchildren. His grandfather took Steven fishing in the Gulf of Mexico on charter boats after which they enjoyed oysters in bars on the beach. Before they left, his grandmother would say, "Any bad thing that grandpa does to you, you write down here [in a notebook] and we will take care of it when you get back." Steven wrote, "He made me eat tomatoes, he made me eat snails, he gave me a Dutch rub, he gave me an Indian burn," etcetera. Steven remembers his grandmother in the kitchen and his grandfather watching a financial show on the television while reading the Wall Street Journal. To get his attention, Steven and his brother would start jumping off the couch and yell, "Stop grandpa, stop hurting us, ouch, ouch!" Grandma would respond, "Stop that, I'm not going to tell you one more time to stop hurting those children." After a couple of rounds grandma would come in and start hitting grandpa with a rolled-up magazine, telling him to "stop hurting the children." Grandpa defended his innocence while the boys were laughing in the corner. When Steven's grandmother left the room, his grandfather would only look at them and smile. This happened on many occasions.

Both homes were nurturing, safe and secure, leaving wonderful memories for Steven. Both grandfathers were hard workers, self-reliant, problem solvers, devoted to family, lived through the depression so also financially frugal. Steven admired them. Under their love and influence, he learned to be a farmer and woodsman. Both grandfathers had significant impact on cultivating his independence and self-reliance in nature and, ultimately, his decision to enlist and become a U.S. Navy SEAL.

THREE

College and Enlistment

Steven lived with his dad through high school and then left home to attend Miami-Dade Community College in Miami on a swimming scholarship. The coaching was not ideal, so Steven talked to a swimming coach at Broward Community College in Florida and left to swim there. This coach switched him from a free-style sprinter to a breaststroke swimmer which fit him better physically. Steven finished two years of inter-collegiate swimming and left to attend Arizona State—a Division I, top 10 National Collegiate Athletic Association (NCAA) Swim Team. Though recruited by other colleges, Steven was determined to swim for ASU. Years prior, on a multi-family vacation in Arizona, Steven and a high school friend of his looked down on the University's beautiful pool facility; the friend said that Steven could never make it onto the ASU Swim Team—he wasn't fast enough. Then and there, Steven decided that he was going to swim for ASU. He had now reached his goal, but he wasn't content; it wasn't enough.

Steven didn't like college; his only goal was to make the swim team and after he did, he didn't have anything to further challenge him. One day, he and his ASU roommate, a friend that had swum with Steven since his Florida days, decided that they were going to talk to someone about becoming a Navy SEAL. They had discussed "The Teams" since they were in Florida. They went to a local Naval recruiting office in Tempe, Arizona and told the recruiter, in no uncertain terms, that they wanted to enlist in the Navy for the sole purpose of going to Basic Underwater Demolition SEAL training (BUD/s). By the time they left the office, the recruiter was looking into the process of entering the Navy on this track. They were to come back in a few days for testing and to discuss what position they would take to start in the Navy on their way to BUD/s.

They traveled to Phoenix to the regional recruiting center and were administered the Armed Services Vocational Aptitude Battery (ASVAB) test—this is academic testing used to determine qualification for enlistment in the U.S. Armed Forces. Steven and his friend scored so high that they could've picked from any enlisted position in the Navy. Steven's only goal was to pick a position that would be the best route to BUD/s, and in which he would have the freedom to prepare for the physical testing for BUD/s. They went back to the recruiter to discuss which jobs were available and when. They both wanted to go to Corpsman school—Corpsmen are enlisted medical specialist in the Navy—but the training takes too long. They didn't want to go to Yeoman school—Yeoman responsibilities include administrative and clerical work—but it is the shortest and easiest school.

They signed the contract with the NAVY, picked Yeoman school and planned to leave in January—when they would need to go to boot camp to enter positions that would open six weeks afterwards. Steven was scheduled to graduate after the spring semester of that year, but he didn't register; he was completely focused on getting into BUD/s. No opportunities came up until May, so he could've finished college, but he didn't graduate, by one semester.

They left for boot camp on May first of 1994 and it started May second: eight weeks in Great Lakes, Illinois. Steven found boot camp extremely easy, physically, and the academic part not much more difficult. He became the Yeoman for the boot camp company, so he could be on his own most of the time; he could run everywhere he went and would work out in the showers at the end of his shifts—all to prepare for the BUD/s physical training (PT) screening. The guys that wanted to go on to BUD/s took a PT test at week five of eight; eligibility included physical tests, their ASVAB scores and their current positions. Forty men showed up for the "rate check," twenty had a SEAL source rate, only five passed the swimming test, four passed the pull-up test, three passed the pushups, two passed the sit ups and only one passed the run—Steven.

After boot camp Steven went to Yeoman school in Mississippi for three weeks. As with boot camp, Steven was able to be away from his command more than with any other position—he had the most freedom to train for BUD/s. After Yeoman school Steven waited for a BUD/s class to open. He went home for Christmas and when he returned, he went to Coronado, California for BUD/s.

FOUR

Basic Underwater Demolition SEAL training (BUD/s)

BUD/s is six months long. There are a couple of weeks of basic orientation and mostly PT. There are four evolutions per day of physical training: four-mile beach runs, pushups, pullups, obstacle courses, etc. First Phase—Hell Week. Thursday of Hell Week, Steven started to have problems with his esophagus and stomach, and he started coughing and throwing up blood. He tried to hide it, but the instructors saw blood droplets in the sand and "hammered" the class until the person bleeding came forward. Steven was taken to medical; he was hydrated and treated and, still on Thursday, asked if he wanted to join the class again. He put his soaking wet, sandy, clothes back on, returned to his position on the boat and continued. Even though he was gone for only hours he was rolled from class 200 to 201 once Hell Week was secured.

Monday after Hell Week Steven found that he was injured—everyone was banged up from the week so he didn't think much of it, he figured it would just go away. In reality, adrenaline got him through the week, but now the full extent of his injuries was revealed. He woke bloated and scabbed, and had great difficulty getting around; he could hardly walk. He had gone through Hell Week with a stress fracture—he was treated for eight weeks.

Every phase of training has higher standards than the phase before. You work against yourself; you have to beat your own time every time. Steven learned to game the system; he would not fail. At this time, if you didn't make it through BUD/s you were sent to the fleet (a most undesirable position, for him); you had one shot. Steven took it one meal at a time; he only needed to make it to the next meal. They were required to run everywhere, so meals alone were six miles per day.

Phase Two is diving training—from beginning to advanced diving school—open circuit and closed circuit. Open circuit is when the equipment produces bubbles and closed is the advanced part when there aren't any bubbles or any other signs there is someone in the water.

PhaseThree is land warfare. In this phase there are ongoing swimming tests; students swim in pairs. Steven and his partner were placed at number one. A student in the class was failing the swims; the partner of the failing student approached Steven and asked if he would pair with him and help him. The student was from Singapore and if he failed out of BUD/s he would be disgraced in his country; additionally, his family would have to reimburse all of his expenses. He could barely speak the language. Of course, other guys had failed out by this point, but Steven believed this person had what it took to be in the Teams, he was just having trouble with the swimming test; at this point they were almost done with the six-month training.

Steven tied the student from Singapore to himself with a piece of 550 cord and told him to kick as hard as he could. Steven pulled him and the pair came in fourth—he didn't fail. This man still expresses his gratefulness to Steven to this day.

Steven graduated from BUD/s training and went to Basic Airborne School at Fort Benning Georgia. Here he was trained in static line parachuting. Steven passed and earned his Jump Wings. He went back to San Diego for a Combat Fighting Course, a Dive Maintenance course, MX16 to learn how to fix diving equipment, and Seal Delivery Vehicle (SDV) training to learn how to pilot and navigate mini submersibles. The SDV course was the first time

Steven met any foreign operators—British Special Boat Service—who were also being trained in SDV.

FIVE

Survive, Evade Resist and Escape School

(SEAR SCHOOL)

A SEAL's task is to evade capture. SEAR training teaches the men how to handle capture from the enemy, what to expect, how to handle torture and, hopefully, not betray their country. The men are released in the day and given about thirty minutes to hide. Most of the group followed Steven, who had proven to be a leader in his class. He told them that no one would make it to "drop dead time" with the ground looking like a herd of elephants trampled it and to spread out; he then bid them good luck. He and the class officer stayed together. They found the largest elder bush—the thorns were three or four inches—and dug their way under the bush to the middle covering their tracks and digging as they moved under the bush. Then, they fell asleep. Throughout the day, they heard their classmates being found, hooded and taken to a van to be transported to the training site. Late afternoon the instructors, via bull horn, ordered Steven and the class officer to come out; they didn't believe the instructors, so they stayed hidden. They did not emerge until the instructors threatened that they would be discharged from training if they did not come out. When they came out of their hiding location the instructors took them in the same way they had the students who had actually been caught, making it seem as though they had caught them, and not that they had come out voluntarily.

SIX

From SDV Team I to SEAL Team VI

Steven was assigned to SDV Team I, so, in May of 1996, after his required trainings to ready him for this assignment, he left for Hawaii. While here, he went through Dry Deck Shelter training and studied for his Trident Boards. During this year, Steven was awarded the Navy SEAL Trident and the Naval Enlistment Code of 5326; the designation of a combatant swimmer, a.k.a. Navy SEAL. Steven was on SDV Team I, in Hawaii, for almost five years.

SEVEN

Steven Meets Jo

In the fall of 1997, Steven returned home to be best man in the wedding of one of his closest high school friends. The maid of honor was the bride's sister, Jo. Steven met Jo for the first time at the wedding and they fell for one another. He was now established as a Navy SEAL; Jo was a senior in college—they had a shared upbringing in Michigan which made her appealing. *Jo also mirrored Steven's passions and interests.*

Jo convinced Steven that she had plans to be an independent businesswoman which really appealed to Steven. Jo visited during her spring break a few months after meeting at the wedding and the two eloped—they had spent a total of a few weeks together before marrying. Steven wanted to date longer, but Jo *threatened* that if they didn't get married, she was going to take a job in Florida, and *threatened* that the relationship would be over. With Steven only "knowing" her for a short time, not giving him time to "really know" Jo, he agreed, thinking that they were very compatible. In the beginning of a relationship there can be intense lust. She returned home to graduate and plan a formal wedding. Steven did not invite his two closest friends; even then he knew that things weren't right and that his friends would've likely called him out on it. Steven's mother did call him out, but he dismissed her warnings. After the wedding Jo moved to Hawaii.

Steven had already begun the rigorous training for his first deployment before Jo moved in. After she moved in, he finished training and then he began a deployment. This involved a year and a half work up (not continuous, includes individual school, unit level training and leave) and then a six-month deployment to the Middle East. This type of schedule rolls continuously throughout the career of an active duty SEAL.

Jo became pregnant with their first child before Steven's first deployment and within a year of their meeting. Before Steven's second deployment, he put their things in storage. Jo and their son, Thomas, moved to Florida to live with her mother and stepfather. Later, they moved to Virginia Beach to meet Steven following his deployment. Jo became pregnant with their second child a couple of years later while in Virginia Beach.

Steven was assigned to Green Team—a selection and training team—to try and get into the command now known as SEAL Team VI. Following September 11, 2001, Steven was assigned to Blue Team, which is a part of SEAL Team VI. There, he was an assaulter and breacher; he was put on an assault team while his secondary responsibility was as a breacher. Steven had already gone to Sniper School while on SDV Team I, so after only a year, he was sent to a Sniper Cell on Team VI.

EIGHT

Marital Misery

Steven and Jo's relationship deteriorated quickly, but it was possible to keep the family together with him gone the majority of the time. The two didn't spend more than two continuous weeks together until Steven stopped deploying in 2009. When Steven was home, he devoted most of his time to visiting extended family and connecting with his two boys. With no intimacy or connection with Jo, Steven looked elsewhere for companionship and started to engage in unfaithful behaviors. He searched for someone with whom he could develop a real partnership, but no one offered enough for him to break up his family.

Throughout the marriage, Jo's moods shifted between extremes within short periods of time; Steven, not knowing how to handle these shifts, talked to several professionals thinking that she might be bi-polar, seeking help for her and for their family.

Some of her former friends in Virginia Beach told Steven years later they had observed the same behaviors. These shifts were so extreme, they thought she took on different personalities.

Any attempt on Steven's part to try to get help for Jo was met with intense rage. Jo told Steven that it was only menopause. Jo would not get out of bed for days due to migraines, something for which she did not seek help. When Steven was training or deploying, neighbors told him, upon his return, that she and the children rarely left the house. One neighbor commented that the youngest would yell and wave to her from the upstairs attic.

NINE

Destroying the American War Hero

At the start of summer 2004, after a deployment to Afghanistan, Steven arrived home to a list of demands from Jo. Those were the days before decompression stops that helped warriors to acclimate from combat to civilian life. Steven could be engaged in a life-threatening operation and eighteen hours later walk through the front door of his home. Steven decided to end his marriage to Jo: he left. Though the marriage was really over at this point, they spent several more years together, based solely on coercion. Jo threatened that if he did not come back to her, she would take his children as far away as possible and not let him see them; she threatened to destroy his career and to ruin him financially. She went on to threaten that court professionals would believe her; he was damaged and dangerous and she was a loving mom who had sacrificed herself and her needs to take care of the kids and the home while he was constantly away. She was unwilling to work which left Steven to be the sole provider, deploying continually, for too many years. He had no choice, in his mind, but to return to her. He could tolerate a lot in order to not lose his boys. By the end of that summer, he moved back in with her. His return to the marriage under threat gave her power and control, which she exercised; her psychological and verbal abuse escalated toward Steven and toward the children.

Jo began preparations to destroy Steven if he did ever try to leave her. Jo said to Steven (too many times for him to count), "Steven, you will pay for leaving me." Everything that Jo threatened (e.g., job, kids, finances, turning his family and friends against him, ruining his life, etc.) came to fruition.

Years later, after divorcing Jo, Steven started communicating, at different times for different reasons, with two of his former SEAL Team brothers. Catching up with one another, they started to put pieces together and were astonished at the similarities in the behavior of their ex-wives pre- and post-divorce. All three women made false claims of domestic violence and all three made the exact same threats: "If you leave me, I will take your children from you," and "This can all go away if you come back to me." One of the other exes was involved with the defamation of Steven's character, during his divorce, falsely making him out to be the abuser. The other two women wrote letters, with nearly identical information, in each other's divorce cases; Jo also wrote a letter in one of the cases. All three men had very long drawn out and highly litigated divorces. All three found themselves in court often facing surprising and outlandish allegations, all three feared what would come next if they dared to go on the offensive—the allegations were nearly identical. One had to pay so much spousal support that he had to live in a camper, while making a Navy SEAL Officer's salary. In the other's case (where Jo had written a letter), the judge finally saw through the false allegations and things turned around for him. His case was in the lower forty-eight with better resources and more psychologically sound family evaluations than in Steven's case. I contacted an expert in Parent Alienation Syndrome who found us an attorney who offered to take on a class action suit for the three men. All three of these war heroes were hesitant to act because they *feared* being in court again, especially the one for whom his case had turned around; he didn't want to stir anything up with her.

Jo and the other SEAL ex-wives still communicate with one another publicly, and on social media. These three women all made additional and similar false allegations post-divorces, continued to stay hostiley engaged with their ex-husbands, initiated excessive and ongoing litigation, made the same threats about taking the children away and the specific threat that "this will all go away if you come back to me." This *could* all be coincidental—that they all separately have the same sort of personality and made the same threats and decisions pre- and post-divorce.

TEN

Steven Questions Jo's Mental Health

Between 2003 and 2009 Steven noticed that Jo's verbal and physical abuse against his boys was escalating and increasing in frequency. Steven's dad and stepmom commented that they had overheard her harshness toward the boys while they were doing their homework. They also commented on how she verbally abused Steven right in front of them. Jo yelled and screamed a lot. According to Steven's mom, during a visit with the boys sometime after the divorce, Jo screamed at the boys quite frequently. On many occasions, Steven observed Jo yelling at the boys until they cried and even witnessed her slap each of them in the face, also on multiple occasions.

Steven approached Jo's mom about Jo's behavior in late 2008. Not knowing how to handle Jo, he called his mother-in-law and asked if there were any bi-polar relatives or a history of mental illness in the family. She said there was not. Fearing Jo's reaction, Steven asked her to keep his inquiry between himself, her, and her husband, (Jo's stepfather). He feared that Jo would become enraged, knowing how opposed she was to getting help. Jo's mom eventually told her about the conversation and, as anticipated, Jo flew into a rage, stating that there was nothing wrong with her and that she didn't need any help with anything. Steven was genuinely concerned for his boys because when he was gone, Jo was spending the majority of her time with the boys, isolated and alone with them.

Still not knowing what to do, in March of 2009 Steven talked to his command psychologist about Jo's irrational and unpredictable behavior. He approached the same psychologist again in October 2009, voicing his concerns. One minute she was pleasant then, like the turn of a page she became very hostile and verbally abusive to Steven and/or the boys. This psychologist, taking his concerns seriously, offered to arrange for the Judge Advocate General (JAG, military attorney) in San Diego to take a statement if needed. Steven now wishes that he had done more; professionals were available to help.

Steven also talked to a medical doctor about Jo. He spoke with the doctor from his command on multiple occasions (July and October 2009, and January 2010). He described her mood swings, and her abuse toward him and the children. The doctor gave his professional opinion of potential causes and suggested that Steven encourage Jo to seek psychological testing. Steven told him how tired he was living with Jo's abusive and aggressive behavior. The doctor also offered to make a statement to the JAG in San Diego. Later, he offered to testify during the divorce trial about his consultation with Steven and the fact that Jo's medical records, following her claim of domestic violence were inconclusive. Steven was poorly represented; his attorney, for some reason, did not call upon the doctor for testimony, though the doctor waited by the phone.

ELEVEN

The Ketchup Bottle

An example of when Steven was particularly disturbed by Jo's often extreme, abusive and irrational behavior occurred during dinner one evening. Steven and Jo's six-year-old son, Jay, was playing with the plastic cap on a ketchup bottle. Jo told him to stop. When the cap finally snapped off, Jo stood up in a rage, took the plastic bottle of ketchup, poured a large amount of ketchup into her hands and rubbed it into Jay's hair (as though it was shampoo) then she smeared it all over his face. Steven, shocked, and not knowing what to do, began recording the incident on his cell phone.

> *Jo: I warned you, I take the time to do what I do and you ruin my stuff, I'm sick of it.*
> *Steven (to Jo): Is he alright?*
> *Jo: Oh he is fine; he is just shocked I did it.*
> *Steven: I can't believe you did that.*
> *Jo: Are you kidding me?*
> *Steven: No, I am not kidding you.*
> *(Jay crying in his room)*
> *Steven: That was kinda—*
> *Jo: Kind of what?*

Steven: Over the top.
Jo: Are you kidding me?
Steven: No, I am not.
Jo: Are you kidding me?
Steven: Rubbing ketchup all over your kid's head, you do not think is over the top?
Jo: I warned him, if he breaks it I would rub ketchup on his face; I told him that. So, he took the lid and cracked it open and broke it. So, what was I supposed to do? Not do it?
Steven: I don't think I would have come up with a punishment that, hey I am going to rub ketchup on your face if you do that.
Jo: Well (Jo putting food into her mouth) I should of rubbed his face in it. The same kind of thing you do with a dog, right! Rub its face in it! Or a cat.
Steven: You are going to compare your son to a dog or a cat.
Jo: Yeah, I am right now, because let me tell you how much shit he breaks around here, or gets his little nose into and he gets away with it. So if you have a problem with it you debate it with me at a different time and a different place.
Steven: I just think that is a bit extreme.
Jo: (while eating) I warned him, he made the choice, he did it. You want me to go and buy a new ketchup?
Steven: Did he really do it?
Jo: Yes! I watched him! Right here go like this, and peel it right off, that's harmless. (Jo continuing to eat.)
Steven: Where is he? (Steven then left the room to go to check on him)

Jay was laying in his bed sobbing and was still covered with ketchup. It was burning his eyes. He had it up his nose and in his ears; he was covered. He was crying hard, the kind of cry that makes it difficult to catch your breath. Steven held him and calmed him back down. Steven felt so badly for him and for his brother who had witnessed this abuse. Jo offered no help in cleaning up Jay and offered no apology. This incident is a typical example of Jo's manner in dealing with people: Jo thinks she is never wrong; Jo is always the victim (even when with her 6-year-old son) and Jo always knows best. In hindsight, Steven feels that he should have immediately called social services and he regrets not taking action. Steven was trained to be a warrior, was not familiar with the field of social work and knew nothing of social services nor of his rights as the children's father—the war hero was not trained to deal with this level of mental illness and abuse.

When Steven's attorney brought this incident up during their divorce trial, Jo said that she had laughed about it with Jay and that it was no big deal—her attorney quickly dismissed the matter. What adult with sound mind would laugh at any time about an incident like this? It's puzzling that Jo and her attorney found child abuse funny—that it could be laughed about with the abused child. Steven later commented to his attorney that if he would have taken a bottle of ketchup and rubbed and smeared it on her attorney, he would've been in contempt of court and charged with assault, but this behavior is laughable for a child? Jo's attorney, making light of this abuse, should also be held accountable, professionally, for putting a child at risk of further abuse. One does not engage in this level of violence randomly, nor only one time. Days, weeks and months with no accountability, violence escalated. Abusers who are not caught test their limits.

TWELVE

The False Domestic Violence Allegation

In January 2009, just prior to his final overseas trip in support of the Global War on Terrorism, Jo yelled at Steven, "I hope you don't make it back from this trip!" He asked, "You want me to die?" Jo asked him to increase their life insurance policy by one and a half million dollars, antagonized him with threats, and started arguments to unsettle him and to leave him vulnerable, right before he engaged in life-threatening operations.

In the summer of 2009, giving his marriage one last try for the sake of his children, Steven moved his family. He took a position in Alaska, one that did not require deployment, allowing the family to spend time together. The trip to move to Alaska for Steven's new position, by car, was the longest continuous time that he and Jo had ever spent together, and he could not endure her abuse any longer. By the end of the trip, he contacted an attorney to file for divorce as soon as possible (after the mandated six-month waiting period). Six months later, in January 2010, Steven asked for a marriage dissolution and scheduled an appointment with a JAG in order to keep legal fees to a minimum. In February, before leaving for a training trip, Steven gave the completed paperwork to Jo. He finished his part about what he thought was fair for splitting finances and time with the boys and asked her to fill out her part while he was gone. They would then see the JAG and mediate a divorce decree when he returned from his trip. She said, *"This is not how it is going to happen."*

When Steven returned home from the trip, Jo was highly agitated and acting strangely—she was making aggressive eye contact, staring at him continually. She had not filled out any of the paperwork. She had been drinking the night of his return; Steven had decided to not drink anymore following his request to dissolve the marriage, so that she could not use it against him. Jo demanded that Steven review a book about divorcing in the military, specifically looking at retirement calculations. She put the book in his face, then hid it behind her back and started toward the stairs—ignoring him when he asked to see it. Steven followed her, asking to look at the book. As she turned a corner at the base of the stairs Steven tried to smack her on the buttocks to get her attention. He reached around the wall separating the stairs from the bottom floor, his forearm caught on the wall, so he barely touched her. She continued up the stairs, so Steven sat back down on the couch to watch the Olympics, recovering from his training trip. She went into the room where the children were playing and started to become hysterical, involving them. He went up to the room to check on her and he asked her if they should tell the boys the title of the book in order to let them know what was going on (the boys indicated that they were annoyed at them—they were interrupting their video game). Jo responded so irrationally and emotionally that he thought it was best to leave her alone.

The next day, Jo seemed fine. She and Steven did not talk about the previous evening. She did not show any fear of him. Steven generally worked out in the garage, showered and left for work before Jo got out of bed. When Steven went upstairs on this morning, following his workout, Jo was up and in the shower herself, which was unusual. The shower is a very small stand up shower—

there is a separate bathtub—this was an attempt to seduce Steven, not just thrifty water usage. Steven did not notice anything different about Jo's body. If she had been bruised the night before, the bruises would have been clearly visible by this time.

Jo did not complain of any injury and was clearly pursuing communications with him while he was getting ready for work. Steven recalls what she said and her body language was flirtatious, and she in no way seemed afraid of or angry with Steven. Considering the events of the prior evening, her curiously abrupt transition into seductress and his desire to get out of the marital relationship, Steven *ignored her* and went to work.

Later in the day, while Steven was at work, he was served a Protective Order. Local authorities escorted him out of the building, where he was the Senior Enlisted Advisor, and took him home. They instructed him to gather his things; he would not be allowed to return home nor to see his children until further notice. Jo had accused him of beating her the night before.

If this accusation had been substantiated Steven would have been dishonorably discharged because he would have not been allowed to carry a firearm. Steven was not arrested, and the case was *never investigated*.

During their highly litigated divorce proceedings, Jo stated several times *"this can all go away if you [Steven] come back to me."* Because of this unsubstantiated accusation and because Alaska lagged behind the rest of the country in understanding psychological issues, Jo was given sole custody of the children, which gave her even more power and control. Jo stayed at their home on Kodiak Island, unnecessarily, even past the start of the boys' school year in Florida. She told Steven's colleague's wife that Steven would never leave her—even as the truck was packed for a military move and the ferry scheduled. Up until the move, she regularly sexted Steven and invited him over to the house—he *ignored* the texts and would only respond to logistics about the boys or the house. She contacted his superiors, saying that he was stalking her, that he would park outside of the house to watch her. Steven found out about these false allegations because his Officer in Charge at his command believed her and confronted Steven.

Jo followed through on her threat to separate Steven from his children, taking them to Florida. Any time that Steven was in the area, Jo could make further false allegations; he could not go near his children for fear of her fabricated claims.

Jo was always opposed to any sort of therapy for herself or the boys. The few times that she saw a therapist, Steven believes was in order to document her false domestic violence accusations. These are the only times that Jo "sought help"—coincidentally at the same time as her accusations. Jo blocked all of Steven's attempts to provide professional help to his boys during the difficult divorce. The court's initial order demanded that Steven see his boys for a few hours a day—under the condition he take them to see a professional therapist while visiting them in Florida for Christmas break 2010. Jo even tried to sabotage this. Jo refused to allow the boys to participate in the court-ordered therapy with the therapist that Steven selected, and she refused to participate herself. After he left Florida, she found a different therapist for the boys, but only took them a few times. Because Jo had sole custody, therapists were not able to meet with the boys without her consent, something she would not give.

The Findings of Fact and Conclusions of Law in the Divorce, October 2011, include the following: "The court is concerned about what happened at Christmas time in Florida. It doesn't appear that Mrs. Brown did everything in her power; that Steven could have had a lot of time with the kids…The court is concerned about the statements from the children to the custody investigator. The children would not know about this without a parent saying something to them."

During the nearly two-year period of courtroom battles before the final trial, the false allegations morphed into Steven punching Jo in the lower back. She claimed to have sustained very serious injuries, but the hospital "lost her x-ray." She claimed to neighbors and friends in both Alaska and Virginia Beach that the incident included a black eye; different stories with different people. The stories changed according to the attention that Jo received or did not receive. Steven later learned from many of her previous friends and neighbors that the longer you listened to Jo the more elaborate the stories became—like oxygen with fire.

An affidavit, in the form of a letter to the court, supports Steven's joint custody of his boys. By this point, he had been fighting for joint custody for four years. Before each visitation, Jo took matters to the courts to fight for less visitation (or none at all) for Steven. The writers were Steven and Jo's neighbors for nine years when he was stationed in Virginia Beach.

7/30/2014

I have been asked by Steve Brown to make a statement about my experiences in my relationship with Steve Brown and Jo Brown and their children, Thomas and Jay.

Steve and Jo moved next door to my husband and me in December of 2002. At first Jo kept to herself and I did not get to know her until we met at the kid's bus stop. My first impression was that she was over protective and very controlling. If the kids did not want to wear the coat, hat, or gloves she wanted them to wear at the bus stop she would grab them by the coat around the neck and shake them tell them they must wear them, even when all the other kids were not wearing the big coats, hat and gloves. When Thomas and Jay took off their backpacks and tossed them on the ground in line with the other kid's backpacks, just as the other kids had done, she would grab them around the neck of their clothing and tell them that "they better not bend their binders." I always felt this was a little extreme. The kids always seemed as if they had been having a bad morning.

Jo and I became friends over the years, even though I was a much older mother than her, we did have two boys the same ages and we were both stay at home mothers, so we did talk quite often. Jo always portrayed Steve as an unloving husband, and I felt Jo and Steve did not have the best relationship. I knew she loved her boys just as I knew and observed Steve loved his children. I never witnessed Steve do anything violent to Jo or the boys. It was obvious the marriage was not a happy one.

In 2004 Jo told me and one of our other neighbors that Steve told her he no longer loved her. He told her he loved her as the mother of his children but did not love her as a wife. We all felt sad for her, but we were not at all shocked because of all the signs and stories Jo would tell.

A few neighbors and I would hear stories about emails Jo had found of Steve and other women. We would also hear how he totally did not respect her or treat her right. I thought that Steve was a terrible person, and I wondered why he didn't just leave her. I also could not figure out why Jo would want to live that kind of life.

I spent many hours listening to stories about Steve and how unfaithful he was and how terrible he was. I found myself not liking him. But never did I witness anything abusive or hurtful toward Jo or Thomas and Jay. She would tell me she was going to confront him about emails from other women and that she was going to give him a choice to stop or leave. I was always concerned and sad for her because of these stories. But what was strange to me is that I would spend a good part of the day hearing all the details and stories, and the next day when she was supposed to give him the "talk," she would act as if everything was fine; as if nothing had ever happened. I did not want to pry or push her to talk about it, but she acted as if it never happened, and all was just fine. Which made me concerned and wondering how much of what I was hearing was truth or made up.

Most of the neighbors who had heard these stories could not understand *why she would not except that her marriage was over and move on, especially after she had been told by Steve that he no longer loved her.*

She did expect a lot from the boys, perfect school work and she kept them indoors most of the time unless it was baseball season. We live on a street with many boys who are Thomas and Jay's ages, all the kids were always outside playing games; one of the favorite games was street baseball, which was played right in front of the Brown house. Jo would keep Thomas and Jay indoors. When asked if the boys could come out, she would say "they had schoolwork to do, or were doing something else indoors." Jay would call out to me from the upstairs window and say, "Hi Mrs...." They did spend a lot of time playing video games and they were quite good at it. All this mostly happened while Steve was away on duty or not home.

I felt so bad for them, that they could not go out and play like all the other kids. Many of the neighbors felt the same and commented to each other about this. Thomas and Jay were allowed out to play if Jo came out and visited outside with other neighbors. Jo did not like Thomas to touch trees or pet dogs because she told him he was allergic to them. It seemed she wanted to keep them in a bubble, that the outside world was dirty and could be harmful.

Even though I knew all this, I still liked Jo and considered her a friend. In 2009 Steve took a job in Kodiak Alaska and they moved. I still spoke with Jo on the phone and she still talked about how Steve was uncaring. She told me she was going to a counselor in Kodak telling them about Steve. She said she was setting up all she needed for divorce and letting them know what a terrible person and that he was an alcoholic. She told me that he suffered PTSD and that she was getting all this documented and put on his record. She also told me she wrote to the Oprah Winfrey show and wanted to be on the Oprah show to talk about women and their husbands who suffered from PTSD from the war. I still spent many hours with her on the phone hearing about this.

One night she told me that Steve found out that she was reading a book on "How to Divorce in the Military," and he wanted to see the book. She did not want him to see the book, so she ran with it upstairs, and Steve followed and "slapped her on her bottom." She asked him to stop, and that was the end of it. Then I heard that she told my neighbor across the street that Steve beat her on the bottom and gave her a black eye. I thought this was funny because I spoke with her the night before and there was never a mention of being beaten or hit in the face. She also told me that due to this slap on the bottom she suffered a spinal injury and numbness to her fingers.

The stories grew larger and more dramatic and I always asked her, "What does your mother think of this?" Because if all this was true, and Steve was beating Jo, I would think her parents would be there as soon as possible to help her. This is when I started getting suspicious and wondered how much is real and how much is made up. It seemed to me Steve did not love her as he told her in 2004, and Jo did not want to accept it, and now things were getting desperate.

After she moved to Florida with Thomas and Jay to stay with her mom and stepfather she had asked me if she could come and stay with me a for five days because she wanted to go to a friend's birthday party and that she needed to renew her military ID and take care of a few things. I was glad to have her come and stay, and I figured she deserved a break. She had told me she was going to go to Steve's old command at Dam Neck and tell them what Steve has been doing to her and that he had stolen government property. She said they did not like him and that they did not want him to come back to Dam Neck.

During the time Jo was back here in Virginia Beach and staying at my house, I noticed a side of Jo I have never noticed. She seemed determined to get back at Steve and was going to be sure everyone that they both knew, knew what a terrible person Steve was. I felt like Jo was not the person I thought she was, and I was starting to realize that most and maybe all she had been telling me was fabricated.

I did not hear from Jo for about 2 months after she returned to Florida, until she called me asking if I could make a statement about her being a good mother to her attorney. I told her that I really needed to let her know how I felt, that I felt that she seemed to have had a specific agenda while she was in Virginia Beach and spending time with her old neighbors/friends, who had been listening to all her stories of how terrible of a person Steve was for all these years, was not part of her agenda.

Even after hearing this from me she still thought all was well with us, and she could not see any problem. Jo would not accept what I had to say and made no apologies, as you would think one would, if you were truly a friend. And that was the last I have ever heard from Jo Brown. It seems I am no longer of any use to her.

To be honest, I am glad, because I feel she is unstable and needs to get *professional help. I am afraid that because she cannot control Steve and the loss of her marriage, that she will do anything possible to get revenge, even if it is not in the best interest of Thomas and Jay.*

It is always sad when a marriage ends and children must be shared with two parents separately, but I would hope and pray that adults could put aside their emotions and do what is right for their children.

I have seen Steve with his boys, and I know he loves them dearly and know he would only do the best for them. I know the boys love both of their parents. I have no doubt that Jo loves her children. I do not believe that the children are afraid of Steve and I believe Thomas and Jay would benefit from having joint custody.

Thank you.
The Neighbors

During the time period that the neighbors have documented, Jo begged Steven for another child; she wanted to try for a girl. This caused serious disagreement within their relationship. Steven was in the relationship due solely to Jo's threats; he did not want another child with her. He believed that she would trick him into having sex at times that she knew she was fertile; this is known in the scientific community as "reproductive coercion." Steven scheduled a vasectomy and told Jo about it the day of the surgery so that she could drive him to the procedure. She was furious. He confronted her about what he believed she was doing, and told her that he, without question, did not want another child with her. A vasectomy is not advised at his (then young) age, but he was sure; he knew that if he remarried one day, he could reverse the procedure. His personal decision for a vasectomy was the subject of arguments all the way up to the time of the final separation.

THIRTEEN

Normal People don't make False Allegations: That is the Lowest

"We can never serve a child's best interest by denying him or her the love and affection of a parent who has himself been victimized by a lie."
~*Dr. D. Patterson, The Other Victim: The Falsely Accused Parent in a Sexual Abuse and Custody Case*

Jo's actions are worse than those of a perpetrator; because of false allegations like hers, judges cannot simply believe those that are true victims. Her actions, and those of people like her, cause breakdowns in the judicial systems meant to prevent violence and death. That her false allegations have been validated to such a degree is appalling; she shows no signs of victimization by Steven. On the contrary, she shows signs of being an aggressor and the perpetrator of the abuse. After a verbal assault, as with a true victim, Steven becomes nearly paralyzed with fear of the consequences of standing up to Jo, and he sinks into a depression very unlike his normal behavior. He avoids her as much as possible and recoils and avoids any discussions about Jo. He is filled with anxiety every time he opens email, wondering what she will do next. An abuser remains on the offensive, pursuing the victim and trying to upset the victim's internal balance, as Jo does to Steven; the abuser hurts the victim and takes what is dear to him/her.

A truly abused individual does not coerce their abuser into more communication. Jo's obsessive desire to get Steven's attention, or that of anyone remotely connected to him, runs exactly counter to a victim's response. Victims and survivors of domestic violence do not want to talk about their abuse and most definitely do not want to talk to their abuser; victims are frightened by their abusers, and communications cause unwanted triggering of the past.[1]

Often, it takes years for victims to identify abusive behaviors because victims blame themselves, absorbing the verbal and psychological abuse and, in turn, devaluing themselves. Victims are re-traumatized in the courtroom as the perpetrator enjoys the contact and control, and the victim is forced to endure abuse in this new way. A victim does not initiate any unnecessary legal action for these reasons.

Steven and Jo had been separated for more than a year when he learned from Jay that he had, with Thomas and Jo, just celebrated Steven and Jo's wedding anniversary; exchanging wedding anniversary cards and having a special night. He found this information troubling because what Jo said and did during the excruciatingly long and bitter divorce process ran completely contrary to this celebration. This anniversary party was also very confusing for Steven's boys; they thought that the divorce was complete when Steven first moved out of the house. This antic furthered Jo's agenda to make Steven into the bad guy. During this time, Jo also sent out "Brown Family" Christmas cards as if nothing was amiss.

Jo communicated with (and attempted to communicate) with Steven far more after he handed to her marriage dissolution papers than at any time during the marriage. This action, to Jo, was the biggest *rejection* by Steven; the finality of this action and his detachment was worse than his previous departures.

It's harder for male victims; our system can barely keep up with violence against women, much less *investigate and believe* the claims of abused men. Jo turned the table, presenting herself as the victim. Steven had no chance. He even encountered opposition from within his closest circles because of Jo's tenaciousness for his destruction and because of their more-than-willing ears and interest.

In 1987 two psychologists came up with three psychological profiles for falsely accusing mothers, drawing from their experiences evaluating families for family court.

> "Falsely accusing mothers tend to present as 'fearful victim,' 'justified vindicator,' or to some degree psychotic. The 'fearful victim' presentation involves manipulation of social image around a specific theme to which others respond with sympathy and support, such as child abuse or spousal abuse…mothers in all three categories tend to be histrionic in presentation, so emotionally convinced of the 'facts' that no amount of input, including from neutral professionals, can dissuade them from their perceptions [1]."
>
> "The 'justified vindicator' initially presents as organized and assertive, outraged by the behaviors of the other parent, but if questioned about details will become hostile and may threaten to sue or make ethical complaints against the evaluator/counselor [1, 2, 3, 4, 5, 6]."

In the Findings of Fact and Conclusions of Law in the divorce, the following was included: "Mrs. Brown presents a lot of pictures in Exhibits B, C and D. The defense has said the photographs were not dated and is not sure when they were taken. The black eye is clear; the bruising on her body is clear. The court does not find that the photographs were doctored up, or pictures of other injuries that were sustained by other accidents, but rather sustained at the hands of Mr. Brown. It is enough to trigger a finding of history of perpetuating domestic violence."

The doctor to whom Steven had confided his concerns about Jo's mental illnesses had agreed to testify about these pictures and make a statement that they were inconclusive and could not be used to verify domestic violence—these were pictures that Jo had taken of herself—not those taken by police nor by medical professionals, though both agencies were involved.

Having had black eyes and many other injuries, myself, inflicted as a result of domestic violence, I have a unique perspective on these photos. Jo has sunken eyes; in many of her social media photos her eyes look bruised in the corners. The "black eye" is symmetrical between both eyes, there is not any swelling or additional markings. The photos are extremely grainy, and one showing bruising is in black and white.

All of this reinforced and endorsed Jo's idea of herself as a victim, and of Steven as the perpetrator. This false initiation of Jo's aided her in being awarded sole custody. The court's response made it impossible for Steven to gain joint custody, considering his job responsibilities (he would've had to travel to Anchorage for year-long domestic violence therapy because Jo's "therapist" happened to be the only domestic violence therapist on the island, thus creating a conflict of interest).

Jo and the boys were "effectively protected" from Steven.

An American war hero—a warrior-who engaged in hundreds of life-threatening missions to protect our homeland—found his greatest threat living in his own home.

FOURTEEN

Hell Hath no Fury.....Jo turns her Vengeance Toward me

When Jo learned about Steven and me as a couple, her abuses began to include me. I spent over 400 hours combing through Jo's emails. The redundant and lengthy emails came overwhelmingly to Steven, disrupted his life and interactions with his boys—her ramblings caused Steven to go sometimes months without any communication with his boys. The following emails to him are excerpts, quoted exactly. I have retained spelling and grammatical errors as they speak to her manic typing, and/or drunkenness, impulsivity and/or mental state. She jumps often from talking TO Steven to talking ABOUT him, to attorneys, who are often copied. This tendency appears in all of Jo's emails referenced in this book.[1]

Email 12/13/2011

[Steven and Jo separated in February 2010, and had been formally divorced in May of 2011].

"...They are uncomfortable with you doing this and don't want to share their

time with you between another kid and a girlfriend... They asked me to write this note to you. I hope you understand and listen to them and respect how they feel. They just don't want to be pressured into having a relationship with her. Give them some time...."

Email 12/3/2012
"*Where will they be staying? If traveling back to your girlfriend's, will the boys be staying there? Where might they be sleeping with all her roommates. Will the boys be expected to room in the closet with her son?....Might I remind you of every past instance where you have not done as court ordered and given the itinerary.*"

Email 12/30/2012
"*....or are we confusing our case with your girlfriend's again who clearly in KY would have a parent coordinator or a mediator, especially if a lawyer has not been hired. (I know law, remember) Or are we mistaking your girlfriend as the mediator because I can clearly see you continuing to pull from what I assume is her case when you reference things. And I severely hope that you are not referencing her as a mediator or parent coordinator in this. That could get you in some trouble, as I remind you how cordial I have been.*

....Once again, let me remind you that your complaints do not even hold a candle to the fire that has already been lit and the continued sincerity I have for working amicably to repair your relationship with our children."

Not knowing what else to do, both Steven and I attempted to file Emergency Protective Orders against Jo's harassing and threatening behavior. Considering the volume of motions against Steven in his divorce case, her uncensored *fearless* rages in pages of emails, text messages and phone messages—where she was obviously intoxicated, slurring words and cursing—it seems that if Steven were abusing Jo, she would not hesitate to find her voice within the legal/criminal system.

The EPO was not issued because in Alaska, at that time, there were no cyber stalking laws; only physical abuse was recognized. I was not granted an EPO in Kentucky because Jo is not a relation, as mandated in Kentucky. Judges in both states expressed their desires to help us despite the fact that they could not.

In an email on December 30, 2012, Jo sent:
[The email follows a notification to both attorneys that Steven is being prevented from Skyping with his boys, as the court has ordered. Jo wanted to call or text Steven, but Steven was not comfortable communicating with her by phone or using texting because of her inability to stop, verbally and psychologically, abusing him. He wanted to utilize email, to slow the conversation down, prevent escalation, and document her abuse toward him along with the sheer volume of her communications. This is typical in hostile divorces.]

"....Otherwise, do not harrass, threaten or bully me, or Thomas and Jay. We have had enough. Your command [meaning Steven's superiors at work] *has been in continued contact with me and I will not hesitate to inform them of this. Your continued actions are par for the course for me and continue to get worse, but for the boys, they are young and still have hope. It is time to Stop being a part of the problem and start being a part of the solution. Jo."*

This particular quote is part of a five-page, single-spaced hostile rant against me and Steven. Jo makes unsubstantiated, outrageous assertions and threatens directly and indirectly that if he allows his children to interact with me, she will withhold communication and visitation.

Steven submitted this response to the court in his appeal for emergency protection from her abuse, using primarily the email above:

"Because it is so difficult for society to accept that a man might be abused by a woman, and because she has already asserted, unsubstantiated domestic violence, I will provide documentation, and am happy to provide full emails, or more information upon request. I take her threats very seriously as she has already made at least three attempts, to my knowledge, to take my livelihood and cost me an almost 20-year career. She has falsely accused me to authorities,

my superiors, friends, family, and neighbors of things I couldn't imagine. Things I was shocked to even hear. Jo threatens to have documentation and witnesses, but her being a woman and me in the military, she has been able to simply state that I am harassing, stalking, bullying, threatening and she is believed without question.

I also submit the attached document (emails) to provide some evidence of a pattern of verbal and psychological abuse so that her above threat will be taken seriously. I could talk about incidents occurring within the marriage or abusive phone calls but thought it would be better to simply provide actual documents where she verbally abuses me and now my fiancé. With my impending wedding, Jo's abuse toward me is escalating. Also, my fiancé feels very threatened and fears Jo's potential actions toward her or her children. Evidenced with emails, Jo demonstrates ongoing systematic monitoring, analyzing and interpreting all interactions I have with my sons. The amount of information she claims to know would mean Jo was monitoring and evaluating all interactions I have with my sons: phone, Skype and even visits up to eight weeks. During visits with my sons Jo attempts to involve herself continuously, then analyses visits as if she were there every minute knowing everything. After interactions she interprets how I think, feel and act; how the boys think, feel and act; how everyone else involved thinks, feels or acts; and then proceeds to explain how it would have been handled better by her, all the while hurling accusations and outrageous lies. I believe she is seeking complete control over me, my sons, our interactions, even who is on the other end of one hour a week of Skyping. And if she feels she's losing control (my girlfriend becoming my fiancé) she will resort to desperate measures to regain that lost control: my job, threats against my fiancé, threats to not send the boys for visits unless I abide by her rules. Her desperation to communicate more with me is likely a desire to control me through abuse, evidenced with email documentation, and to triangulate my relationship with my boys (e.g. if I have to come to her for her interpretations then I'm not communicating directly with my boys). She puts herself clearly in the middle of our relationship, dictating, dominating, controlling, amplifying issues, creating chaos; she will not leave us alone to simply have a father son relationship. Jo has demonstrated such a degree of hostility, increasing aggression and has the financial resources to engage in extreme measures that could put me or my fiancé in life threatening danger.

Steven was given a hearing with the judge on January 14, 2013, from 4:09 to 4:23. Excerpts from the hearing transcript include:

"This does not meet the statutes…she lives in Florida so this is not a threat of physical imminent injury."

"In cases like this the person with custody doesn't want the other parent to help…this is certainly the case here."

"Reading through emails, Jo is putting up roadblocks to denying meaningful visitation."

The judge uses the word "relief" for Steven three times.

"I felt I owed it to you to have a hearing and you have a face to face explanation…come back if it escalates."

FIFTEEN

Jo's Abuse Toward Steven, In Jo's own Words

"Husband and Wife shall live separate and apart, each at such place of residence as he or she may freely choose, free from all interference, authority and control, direct or indirect, by the other party...."
~*Findings of Fact and Conclusions of Law, from Steven and Jo's Divorce*

I am using the Measure of Psychologically Abusive Behaviors (MPAB), developed by Follingstad in 2011, as a framework on which to hang documentation. The MPAB provides a scale measuring psychological actions at the more extreme end of psychological aggression, (e.g., abuse). I first present the overall category and then indent with the more specific items on the MPBA scale that fit that type of abuse. Jo, by email, has routinely engaged in eight or more of forty-two psychologically abusive actions on a scale that only includes items rated as highly aversive behaviors violating reasonable expectations. She engaged in twenty-six of the forty-two while married and the only reason for the reduction is that she and Steven no longer lived together, and she couldn't abuse him as she did while they were together. The overall pattern of abuse is: statements designed to harm feelings about himself, keep him in an inferior position with her the superior, isolating him from family and friends by making outrageous and fabricated accusations, besmirching his character and attempts to force him into obedience to her by threatening communication and visitation with his boys [7].

Additionally, her coercion of, or expressed desire to coerce-in nearly every communication, Steven to call and text, according to significant scientific literature, runs exactly counter to a victim's response. There is a desperate tone in her writings for him to call or text—*to not ignore her—to give her attention*. If he had abused her, as asserted, she would want to have as little contact as possible. Steven asked repeatedly for the verbal and psychological abuse to stop while trying to co-parent; she could not, leaving him no choice but to ask her to only communicate with him by email and to no longer call or text him unless it was an emergency.

In an attempt to decrease the amount of chaos surrounding an upcoming visitation, Steven sent this email to Jo on 5/28/2012:

"Jo,

This email is to provide you with communication guidelines for the boy's visit here in Alaska. I believe the nearly continual communication at Christmas was distracting of the boy's limited time with me and chaotic. I would like to be pro-active in providing structure for communication. As their father, it is important that I set clear and established boundaries, so they are free to enjoy their time with me and feel comfortable with my approach to parenting. Per court orders, the boys are to have reasonable contact with the other parent while in the care of the custodial parent. Daily contact is not only more than what I have been afforded, while the boys have been in your care, but reasonable. They will contact you between 7:00pm and 7:30pm AST every day.

According to established co-parenting guidelines (attached), I will contact you with any emergencies, by phone or text, depending on the circumstance. Other than that, if you have concerns you can email me, once a week and I will respond to any legitimate concerns. I will not respond to accusations, hostility, or other verbally abusive comments/statements. I will, however, be willing to respond to straightforward, reasonable, rational and adult concerns and questions you might have, once per week, via email. Please refer to the attachment. These are guidelines developed by a professional mediator/parent coordinator/family therapist.

I have also been a parent for 13 years and additionally been responsible for the development, and lives, of hundreds of young men. The boys will be safe and well parented during their time with me.

Thank you. Steven"

Her immediate response, which dismissed his concerns and request completely:

"As for addressing any concerns with the boys. All concerns are important and are always expressed in an appropriate manner. Therefore, any concerns or subject matter pertaining to both Thomas and Jay, should be address promptly and not on a weekly basis."

Jo did not respect Steven's continued plea for boundaries and to simply abide by court orders, to let him see his boys without interference and simply leave him alone.

I. Controlling Personal Decisions

A. Tried to demand obedience to orders that he/she gave as a way of establishing authority over you.

Email 6/12/12

"I also know that your girlfriend is coming shortly. I can assume this is the person you are having a hard time telling the truth about when it comes to Jay flying home. I am unsure why you can't just come out and say that she will be getting Jay to Anchorage. We are adults here. Unless, you know this is probably the wrong way to see your son off. You should be with him to Anchorage and see him off. That's the right thing to do. Being Jay's parent, it is important to know that he's safe and that you have a plan for him for his trip to Anchorage and layover, and to know the details because you are supposed to

keep me informed way before he travels. So, please send me the details. Not a big deal."

Email 7/5/12

"Unless you have another plan, you are supposed to inform me.... Remember?

You need and are court ordered to give me the details."

Email 9/12/12

"Now, here are few things that I would like to see:

1. Obviously better communication. If I contact Steve in anyway relating to the boys, a prompt and respectable response would be great. If you need to talk to me or inform me of anything, please text or call me. That's fine. I have no problems with that. If you email, you might not get a quick response as if texting or a phone call. I don't get notified on my phone everytime an email comes through. That would be distracting and therefore, I check it when I can during the day.

2. Steve needs to respect that the boys are involved with activities that vary in days and to understand that if there is a problem, we will let him know in good timing before the scheduled Skype time. Then we can work out another time. And the same goes for you, Steve. Please let ME know if any problems arise for you, and we can work out another time, instead of a few times ago hearing from you after the Skype session. Waiting is not very fun for the boys.

3. If by chance, as I have stated to Steve before, that if we are not on Skype or there is a problem in communicating that arises (ex. As happened with the hurricane when the electricity was out), I will text, email as quick as possible to let you know as I did in that situation. Once again, your prompt response of acknowledgement would be greatly appreciated instead of acting like you did not receive the text or email. You most certainly see the texts, because you use your cell phone to call."

B. Examples of coercive attempts (to coerce Steven into calling and/or texting her):

Email 3/27/2012

"Keep in mind, this is for the boys and their happiness is important. If I *do not receive a response, I will have to believe that this will be another court matter, as with the issues below. It would be nice if we could work this out, but if it is too difficult, then so be it."*

Email 9/6/2012

"You left out a few details to both attorneys. One, FaceTime is just like Skype. I had sent you an email message on Sunday relaying that both boys might not be home at the 8pm time of Skype, but made sure both Thomas and Jay would have their Itouch's with them to FaceTime. You did not respond to this email. (This seems to be par for the course with both my emails and the boys emails/ texts).

Let's move onto Wednesday/ yesterday. First, Steve has still not formally given me his new cell phone number as the court order states. Steve somewhat relayed his new number to the kids, but they are still confused as to how to reach Steve. That is an adult matter and he should not expect the boys to relay that information to me. This makes things quite difficult for both the boys and I to get ahold of Steve. No matter what avenue I or the boys try to contact Steve, whether by phone, text, email, there is never a confirmation as to the message nor a response from Steve. It seems to be a silly game that Steven enjoys playing to make me look bad and intern devalue the boys schedule when there are changes. As immature as the actions may be, I have come to expect the increasing lack of communication from Steve and the difficulties in the way Steve works. On the other hand, now including the boys in this failure to respond to any type of communication, is a lack of respect and cause for the boys to become increasingly disheartened. So needless to say, the boys and I are still trying to find the most effective way to reach Steve and get a respectful response but are left with almost no avenues.

[When Jo would not get a response from Steven, she would send messages from Thomas's phone pretending to be him. The messages were obviously from her and not Thomas.]

Second, Thomas did email Steve at 4:26pm yesterday, notifying Steve that the boys would not be able to Skype due to a dinner they chose to attend. Once again Steve did not respond, so therefore we were not able to workout another option. Instead, knowing he received the email and chose not to respond, he proceeded to try to text and FaceTime the boys after the 8pm Skype time with no regards to their email that was sent. I received an email this morning from

Steve that was apparently sent last night, demanding that I get the boys on Skype. The boys were also almost certain that Steve would be unable to Skype anyways because he was on a boat somewhere. Unfortunately, once again these adult matters are expected to be passed along to me."

Email 11/7/12

"I have plenty of documentation where you do not respond to my texts or emails…I have texted you once before, saying if there is a problem and they do this to let me know….Now, is this all because you are in Virginia and feel you need to put on a show? You know if there is a problem, I am very receptive and respectful of yours thoughts. I have plenty of full documentation on that. Heck, I followed your "summer guidelines", you know the ones you lied to the judge and said I decided on the ridiculous times. You have every opportunity to text or call or email me if you had a problem. My lines of communication are always open…Honestly, Steven, I would like nothing more than for us to be able to speak to one another about the boys and for you to be receptive to their feelings. I would love for you to know what the boys are thinking…Now, I have been overly nice, not saying a whole lot about the shenanigans going on, on that end. As I said, If you want to file a motion, it is your choice. Or, you can tell me kindly what the problem is when it arises via text, email, phone right away and we can work to fix it. I have already told you that several times."

Email 11/14/12

"I will also have it documented: I was told by the boys that you couldn't call or get through and they are unable to reach you after numerous attempts. There is proof of that, plus I have had the boys in the kitchen trying to get ahold of you since 8pm. Apparently, something is going on with your wifi on your end. And I'm sure you understand that texting does not require wifi. I am also aware that you were late for facetime. The kids told me you said that I don't allow them to call. This is certainly not the case. I am also aware that I have two upset boys again. I suppose looking at the text conversation will help me better understand.

Steven, you can text me if there is an issue. I would have not seen your email normally right away, but I have been helping Thomas with his paper among other things. This is how I know our wifi is working…Like I said, I am not sure what exactly has taken place because you chose to not involve me…

…Okay, and I was also just told by the boys that they think that they are not talking to you until Spring Break? I'm hearing things like you are not respecting their wishes or responding to questions. I hope this is not true. And I'm sure the spring break comment is not the case, but I would definitely like to get to the bottom of this… I'm not at all enjoying the sad and angry chatter on this end."

Email 11/15/12

"That is fine, however if we arrive home earlier, than I will send you a text."

Email 12/20/12

"But as usual, there is no response from Steve until after the scheduled Skype time is over."

Email 12/30/12

"They stood their ground with me refusing to Skype. At this point I try to get a hold of Steve via text because this is an extremely important situation and I want to find out what is going on. I truly wanted to work this out. But as usual, there is no response from Steve until after the scheduled Skype time is over.

I want no response to this, only your desire to respect both Thomas and Jay and their feelings. And if this is your wish, You may contact me via phone, text or email to work this out in an adult fashion."

II. Hostile Environment (creation of a conflict-filled environment with expressed hatred/contempt.) This also includes Jealousy and Monitoring

A. Intentionally turned a neutral interaction into an argument or disagreed with the purpose to create conflict.
B. Listened in on phone conversations (Skype)

without your permission as a way to check on you.

Steven asked the court for permission to talk to his children without Jo being involved, knowing that they have the right to talk to him. Skype sessions were monitored, analyzed and used against him—if they happened at all; he had to use Skype because he was going weeks (and sometimes months) without talking to them by phone. Jo created an environment where all communication went through her, this way she was able to interpret their feelings in general and about Steven, and to interpret Steven's feelings toward the boys. By not letting him Skype regularly, the boys had difficulty maintaining attachment to the "real him" and instead were more apt to believe in Jo's "version of him."

Without Steven being able to communicate freely he was not able to discern whether or not the boys had valid concerns which he needed to address with them, or if, instead, they were fabricated by Jo.

Email 9/19/2012

"Both boys have numerous homework assignments and a very large test tomorrow. Please grant there request to schedule another Skype time, both are refusing to get on and this is creating an even bigger disruption in the completion of their school tasks."

Email 10/11/2012

"Steve,
Both Thomas and Jay will be unable to Skype on Sunday. We will be out of town until Monday evening (no school on Monday) and not back at the hotel in time to Skype on Sunday. They will Skype with you Wednesday."

Email 11/7/2012

"I will also give documentation to the courts of every time the boys fight me to Skype, or the amount of times they are upset when they end their Skype call and so on."

Email 11/15/2012

"In relaying this morning to the boys that they would be skyping tonight, I was made aware of some concerns they posed to you and are now posing to me because they are under the assumption you are not listening to them and are purposely avoiding them in texts and not considering their feelings. I'm sure the things that they ask are valid. And I guess I'm not quite sure why you would not answer them unless you know it's going to cause a problem. Apparently, the boys are asking to only talk to you during Skype or phone conversations and it seems to be a topic that is quite bothersome to them. Once again, to me that sounds reasonable that they just want to spend time with you. Skype time doesn't need to be anymore difficult. Please respect both boys. Try to answer their questions truthfully, don't leave them hanging, and by all means please do your best to make them feel comfortable, meaning no unnecessary surprises. They are 13 and 10 and they like to know what they are getting into. Nobody likes going in blind. They, (1) don't like to be fooled and (2) they don't like to be forced into a situations that they have no choice but to go along with and then become upset afterwards. I am in no way, trying to make you feel bad or angry. In fact, you need to know this information in order for you to understand them and get a feeling for what's going on here. Whether you want to believe it or not, your actions have a lasting effect on both boys. It sets the precedent for how they treat future interactions with you. And trust me, I want things to run smooth with you because then things run smoother here. Please, I am asking you kindly to respect both boys wishes."

Email 12/30/2012

"It has occurred to me that the added stress is in relation to Steve's current company staying with him. His girlfriend, Sabrina, is a cause for stress, which I will address later....This just fueled the fire even more when Steve relayed that he noticed the boys were scared to talk on Sunday, which was not the case."

[The boys repeatedly looked up over the computer screen with scared expressions whenever Steven mentioned me or my son.]

"But after Steve's comment, "Give me a call boy!!", there was no way Thomas was getting on. Once again, I could not blame him. This was an extreme situation that had been built up from prior times, that I am afraid that the consequences for both Steve and myself would have far outweighed the boys not skyping, as opposed to them being literally dragged kicking and screaming to the computer. There is no benefit to make the boys do something that causes extreme pain or adds to the pain that they are already feeling. And as a parent, a very good parent at that, I exercised that discretion. It was either let the boys breathe and recover for the next Skype session, or let them carry that bitterness to the next time and so on."

III. Verbal Abuse, Control Personal Decisions And Treat As Inferior:

A. Criticized and belittled you as a way to make you feel bad about yourself
B. Tried to make you think he/she was more competent and intelligent than you as a way of making you feel inferior
C. Treated you as useless or stupid as a way to make you feel inferior

Email 6/3/2011
"I talked with the airline in detail yesterday and had to take care of seat arrangements. They were sitting nowhere near one another. Hopefully in the future this will be done better, but is all taken care of now.
Steve, enjoy these kids. They love both of us and let them do that."

Email 6/4/2011
"I have always trusted your stepmom and have come to her defense numerous times while we were married. It was you and some of your family who did not trust her. It's amazing how these things have gotten jumbled up. This must be one of the many things you have told your family to make them stop talking to me and for the way they feel about my parents. Steven, the boys have been fortunate to be in a very neutral setting and to love and respect everyone. Pleases keep it that way when they visit. The boys did not mistake your words."

Email 6/7/2011

"I would love to be able to come to you as friends /parents of our kids, but when you continue to be dishonest, hiding things, and untrustworthy to myself and even the kids, it is hard not to keep attorneys out of this. I think this time with the kids could be a great opportunity for you to establish some sort of trust with all of us for the future. That is one of the most important things you can do and should be doing. It's not off to the best start. When I ask you a question you should be able to answer it truthfully especially pertaining to the kids. I shouldn't have to ask over and over to get answers. And even then, the answers are so vague or untruthful. Steve, by the time you left the house in Kodiak, we were all terrified of you and so hurt. I had worked so hard in the beginning to repair the boys relationship with you, regardless of what was happening between us; you have no idea. And I continue to this day. It's hard work. You want what's best for you, not for all of us or this all would have turned out differently. If you have everyones best interest at heart then please start acting that way."

Email 10/16/2011

"...The problem is, is that you have never taken responsibilty for any property we have had and now you are getting "caught up to speed". Would you like some cheese with your wine?... "Make sure you put that in your notes as I have done, that you will need to repair that upon pool opening. You are the owner now...

...4. Foundation- You were well aware of the foundation during our presentations of appraisal in court. Waiting on the judges determination of property ownership was essential in the decision on who would be the responsible party. Steve, you are the owner and it sounds like a structural engineer is a good place to start...

...They are deserving of your (you, beginning the owner, given by the judge, meaning that you are now responsible and I have no ties to the property) full payment of deposit of $2800. The [renters of the VA Beach house] are also paid up in their rent. You should have no issues with [renters of the VA Beach house], period.

I do things by the book.

Jo brown"

Email 3/20/2012

"Also, I would like to know their itinerary of their stay with you. This way, there are no surprises like the other trips they have taken to see you. This will make them more at ease. Hopefully this time you will use discretion when making decisions when involving the children."

Email 3/30/2012

"Steve,

As you attempted to address each matter, several issues were still left out. I will write under your responses in a different color.

Jo"

Email 4/20/2012

"I shouldn't have to respond to an email like this but since it concerns the kids and what they are wanting, I will do my best to respond to some of the ridiculousness you have presented. Once addressed, maybe you will stop the tit for tat replies and really focus on what's important; Thomas and Jay's feeling and concerns.

1. You still have not responded to the other concerns.

2. Yes, you haven't been around for the last 2 years, so, no, you really don't know me nor the kids that well. Matter of fact, you haven't really taken the time to know all of us the last, what, 10 years. But the statement you wrote directed to me, "I assume that you would put the boys first, too", seems to be quite contemptuous on your part. I will try to over look that statement, even though you know by my example that I always place Thomas and Jay first, otherwise I would not be addressing all their concerns to you. Afterall, I am fully taking care of them and see to everyone of their needs before mine. You can reserve that statement for yourself.

3. When you speak for the boys, you do realize that is strictly hersay and that they are here with me addressing all these concerns. The animal issue; Thomas, especially, and Jay said they had problems at all the houses in which they had pets, including your mother's. It is not just with cats, it also pertains to dogs as well. Unfortunately, sometimes the kids do not speak up when it comes to you nor are you possibly willing to listen to them as well. But, it is nice to know the dog does not live in your area of the home and that some one is keeping your space clean.

4. I know that you understood clearly that Jay does not want to fly home alone and that Thomas wants to come home with Jay. Your so called solution to this plan with throwing a little of the "You always wanted me to spend more time with the boys", is not going to work nor would it be highly looked upon by the courts. Jay cannot miss school, you know that. Nor would the school be understanding of his rather large amount of days that he would be absent. There are rules to absences and amount of time in the school. Plus, Jay and I know very well what it is like to fall behind and have to catch up on school work. Jay has done this twice before, he does not need to be in that position again for you. It is not a question of whether this is "palatable" for me or you questioning a statement I made when we were married, while you were traveling or choosing to not communicate/ spend time with the boys and I. This is now and this is blatantly a lack of concern for your kid's education on your part. We all know how you feel about school and how unimportant it is to you. You have made that point to both boys this past school year and have left them in tears and very angry with you. Steve, school is important, not just the latter half of highschool. Please feel free to contact the school for a better explanantion……It is not a wise thing for you to tell 2 outstanding students that grades don't matter, because they and I know otherwise. It is also perposterous for you to encourage them to not care about their grades until it is too late. No judge will appreciate kids missing school. Jay will come home before school starts as planned and I suppose I will have to approach my attorney/courts for Thomas.

5. Plane fees: You are able to pay them ahead of time. I asked the airlines.

I try to be an advocate for you or make sure if you said something to offend them, that they know otherwise. It is your actions, words, and example you set, that speak loud and clear to them. I will not advocate for you when you use poor judgement, lie, deceive, hurt, make them feel uncomfortable, etc. I simply redirect them and tell them that you love them. I do not step in the way. I often feel caught in the middle. And if you were more open to hearing what is going on with their thoughts, then maybe things would go much better. Both Thomas and Jay have feelings and should be treated as so, not as property you choose to drag around without considering their thoughts and feelings. Plus, both boys are incredibly busy kids and have very active social lives. We are living very normal lives down here, juggling school, activities and so forth. I am sure that you notice that from the schedules I have sent you."

Email 4/24/2012

"Steve, they do not need to be weighted down with bags for their trip to Kodiak. If you want Thomas and Jay to partake in the things that you stated, please feel free to get those items. We do different things here. Both kids will need new IDs while they are there.

Hopefully, this will set things straight for you and then you can be flexible.
Jo"

Email 12/30/2012

"…or the continued defiance on your part to communicate on itineraries of both boys travel between Florida and Kodiak…Of course there is so much more…steve being behind in child support, stealing from fidelity accounts, canceling insurance, canceling accounts, not paying medical, not paying dental, not paying the remainder of divorce orders, consistently hurting the boys feelings. I could also touch on the complete terror that Steve brought upon us in Alaska and before…all documented…

…Thomas was very stand offish with Steve and both boys were visibly upset. Once again, I had to make light of a situation that continues to plague our home. Steve, you have to be able to see this…And I am quite surprised at some of the texts that have occurred and disheartened by the amount of times you have blown them off not just by text, but also by email…Besides Steve, those are words of a passionate boy who has consistently been dismissed…

…All is ready in hopes you will act accordingly, as I have reassured the boys you adore them and love seeing them.

Sent from Jo brown"

IV. Isolation, Treat As Inferior, Control Personal Decisions

A. Tried to demand obedience to orders that he/she gave as a way of establishing their authority over you
B. Tried to forbid you from socializing with family or friends

Email 5/26/2011

"Lastly, and very important, I would appreciate no surprises for the boys or myself. I expect to be informed as to who will be visiting/ staying in your home (ex. Dad and stepmother, I have heard through the boys they will be there.) while the boys are there. Please respect the boys and only have family there. This time is for you and the boys to be together. I also expect, if you are going camping, leaving the island, leaving the kids with anyone other than you, etc., to keep me informed before it happens. I am still legally responsible for them. We need to be fully honest when the kids are involved. This is the perfect opportunity for regaining some trust and opening the doors up for better communication between us. I am looking forward to that."

Email 6/4/2011

"As for the trip, I know your mom is coming and I am aware that [your dad and stepmother] are coming too, except they are not planning to come to Kodiak? Are you planning on driving around Alaska. I also have been made aware that your travels with the boys have been planned for sometime. It is very important that you speak to me about all this and included your kids in making plans."

Email 6/7/2011

"Please let me know if you are going to be working and what your plans are for the boys if you are doing so. Also, please talk to Thomas about Boston. If you have any questions for me about the trip, I would be happy to answer those. I would like a decision sometime this week."

Email 3/27/2012

"Steve, we will need to discuss this further. We need to work on these dates together and consider the kids as well. This was the order by the judge to work together. Not including the kids in the planning is not fair to them. They do have feelings, that you choose not to consider. I hope you purchased flexible tickets or you will find yourself with some very hurt young men again. You need to consider their schedule. Being a parent doesn't mean you need the boys to make room to fit in your life, but you need to try to fit into theirs…"

Email 11/25/2012

"In the meantime, It would be much appreciated if you could give me a full detailed tentative itinerary of your plans for the trip, including whether you are leaving state lines, daily routine, etc. ; seeing we have had multiple issues with this in the past. The boys have been through enough surprises and stress with travels on your end. I won't hide my concern for the kids safety on issues that have possibly been not brought to your attention. I will certainly try to get to the bottom of some of these issues and if I am unable, I will certainly call upon you for some documentation to insurance these sensitive issues have been cleared."

Email 12/6/2012

"For starters, the Saturday 6:30am flight will need to be changed. We will have to arrive 2hrs early plus travel time to airport and morning routine. The boys will have to get up at 2-2:30am. That's just too early and they won't get a night of sleep. I'll expect your changed flight itinerary soon, as I see that there are more appropriate times the boys should be flying with Delta.

I will also be expecting your documentation on the other matter within the next week so we can proceed.

Jo"

The above email on 11/25/2012 is an excerpt from Jo's communication about my being investigated by social services due to a false physical abuse accusation (of Junior) from my ex-husband, Peter. The case was found to be unsubstantiated, but Jo brings it up in Steven's case (with attorneys) and threatens Steven's visitation.

SIXTEEN

I Hate You....Don't you Dare Leave Me

"The court is concerned, as an aside, whether or not they [the boys] were coached or unduly brought into the divorce as set out by statements made about their Dad wanting the divorce and Mom not wanting it.... Jo was obviously very hurt that Mr. Brown decided he did not want to be married to her anymore."
~Findings of Fact and Conclusions of Law in Steven and Jo's Divorce

Jo "did not want to divorce" Steven, though she strongly asserted otherwise to others and seemed to have more contempt for Steven than for anything else throughout their marriage. According to researchers studying alienated children, extreme alienation of children comes from the beleaguered parent and often the one who opposed the divorce [8].

During Steven's years of visitation with the boys, the boys would tell him that Jo would never marry again, that she was waiting for Steven, that he was lost and the only reason they were divorced is that he wanted it. They also stated repeatedly to Steven that Junior and I were the problem and that if the two of us were gone, their family could be together again.

When Steven returned to the home where Jo lived with the boys, a place that he had not entered without a witness following the domestic violence accusation in February of 2010, so as not to be accused of anything further, he found on every mirror drawings and stick figures of him, Jo and the two boys, some of which had messages. He'd never known Jo to communicate in this way, so these messages were for him. Steven found these messages disturbing.

The most distressing thing about these messages on the mirrors wouldn't be revealed for nearly a decade. In the space below the stick figures images of the family, there is another message specifically for Steven. It is in a wax substance, that we have not been able to remove to date, and can only be seen if there is steam in the room.

Steven kept the house and for years we rented it. Both of us loving Kodiak Island and Alaska overall, we decided to keep it for ourselves as our get-a-way during the summer. It is a great place to detach from daily stressors; it's peaceful and quiet with extraordinary views. Steven works a fishing charter in the summer and Junior works as his deck hand. Steven is also a contractor for the Navy—to offset the cost of keeping the house for ourselves—so that gives me plenty of time to work during the days. Last summer when we were at the house, Steven took a particularly long shower, so the room was steamy. He called for me and I came into the bathroom. He pointed to the mirror; there was writing on the mirror in Jo's hand. I couldn't make out the words. This summer, I took a shower and the words re-emerged—this time I could read them: *"I'll love you forever. I'll love you for always. Forever and always you will be my all."*

SEVENTEEN

Divorce Related Syndromes

"Children in these alignments came to share the views and outrage of the parent with whom the child identified, often the parent who felt abandoned and rejected in the divorce. These children rejected the parent who was perceived as deserting the family, despite a previously close, loving relationship with the parent."
~*Dr. J.S. Wallerstein and Dr. J.B. Kelly, Surviving the Breakup: How Children and Parents cope with Divorce*

In the 1970s, there were significant societal changes especially for women. For example, women began to work outside of the home more than in past decades. There was also a shift in U.S. family courts from the preference in giving mothers sole custody, from "the tender years presumption" to joint custody rulings in the "best interests of the child." This gave to fathers more legal rights to their children and more influence over parenting and custody arrangements. By the late 1970s, high conflict divorces were increasing and family evaluators and court professionals were finding a growing number of cases where parents—most frequently mothers—were programming their children to influence divorce outcomes. Because of this growing concern, the American Bar Association, Section of Family Law, commissioned a twelve-year large-scale study of 700 divorce families to understand the phenomenon that scientists were finding. Clawar and Rivlin published a book in 1991 called *Children Held Hostage*, based on this study, where they describe their findings that divorcing parents were using programming techniques in 80% of the cases, and that even low levels of parental programming had significant impact on children. Also, based on their findings, they came up with the term "psychological kidnapping." Later studies find that as many as 90% of children involved in prolonged custody disputes showed symptoms of Parent Alienation Syndrome [9, 10, 11].

By the late 1980s and early 1990s, scientists found similar results from their studies on disturbing trends in custody disputes. Three divorce-related syndromes emerged from scientists separately, but the etiologies were profoundly similar.

The Medea Syndrome

Medea is the protagonist in Euripides' Greek Tragedy. She kills her children as revenge toward her husband who has rejected her and married another woman (who she also kills). The Medea Syndrome is the modern version of a mother manipulating her own children to inflict pain on their father. The children are taught to absorb their mother's rage as their own feelings and engage in exacting revenge, with her, toward their father, at the expense of the child's normal reaction to divorce—to continue to love and long for both parents [12]. By keeping the target parent hostilely engaged the children remain in the middle of the conflict—a participant in fervently expressing the mother's opinions as their own.

> "Modern Medeas do not want to kill their children, but they do want revenge on their former wives or husbands—and they exact it by destroying the relationship between the other parent and the child…The Medea syndrome has its beginnings in the failing marriage and separation, when parents sometimes lose sight of the

fact that their children have separate needs [and] begin to think of the child as being an extension of the self...A child may be used as an agent of revenge against the other parent...or the anger can lead to child stealing... These parents act out their intense anger in a disorganized but chronically disruptive way which bombards the children, rather than protecting them, with the raw bitterness and chaos of the angry parent's feelings about the ex-spouse and the divorce [12, 13, 6]."

Almost fifty years earlier, psychoanalyst Wilhelm Reich, talked about "parents who seek revenge on the partner through robbing him or her of the pleasure of the child [14]," and in 1980, Wallerstein and Blakeslee found that the children in these cases are overburdened by taking care of the needs of one parent and this disrupts their own psychological development [15].

Divorce Related Malicious Mother Syndrome

"Divorce Related Malicious Mother Syndrome is a disorder where a parent uses an array of tactics including excessive litigation, alienating the child from the target parent, and involving the child and third parties in malicious actions against the ex-spouse. Lying and deception are routinely used. A malicious parent might arrange to have the ex-spouse investigated for use of illegal drugs at work or file a complaint with authorities against the ex-spouse's new partner. Malicious parents are often successful in using the law to punish and harass the ex-spouse, sometimes violating the law themselves but often getting away with it. Their efforts to interfere with the target parent's visitation are persistent and pervasive, including attempts to block the target parent from having regular, uninterrupted visitation with the child and from having telephone contact, as well as trying to block the target parent from participating in the child's school life and activities [16]."

In 1985 child and forensic psychiatrist, Dr. Richard A. Gardner, based on his clinical work with families, introduced the term Parent Alienation Syndrome (PAS) though the phenomenon had been described previously. Parent Alienation Syndrome has become the overarching syndrome; the other syndromes and disorders can contribute to Parent Alienation (PA) without there being full PAS. Though controversial sometimes between various psychology, sociology and anthropology disciplines, the overall consensus regarding alienation of children is that, withstanding child abuse or gross mistreatment, the child must be alienated from the parent irrationally and be a participant in their own alienation; the alienation must be perpetual and not age-related episodes of favoring one parent over the other; for PAS to occur there must be in large measure the influence of the favored parent. The child takes on the themes, emotions and even the language of the alienating parent and becomes the voice against the target parent. PAS is one parent, with the help of the children, "resolving" the divorce impasse by "teaching" those involved who is good, who is to blame and how they should be punished [10, 11].

The SAID Syndrome

At about the same time, and unaware of Gardner's work, researchers and clinical family evaluators Blush and Ross published several papers on the SAID syndrome (sexual abuse allegations in divorce). These two psychologists found a growing number of incidents of sexual allegations in divorcing or divorced families that they were evaluating in their clinical practice. Drs. Blush and Ross were the first to label the phenomenon as the SAID Syndrome,

> "which describes the particular phenomenon which occurs when a sexual abuse allegation develops within a pre-or post-divorce context and when a family unit has become dysfunctional as a result of that divorce process. It is our belief that when sexual allegations in divorce occur (the SAID Syndrome) an entirely

different set of dynamics and variables may exist. These allegations need to be addressed in a discriminately different manner than the sexual abuse allegations in a non-divorcing family [1]."

False accusers are found to accuse others in relationship with the target parent such as a new partner, relatives or stepchildren [17]. Other scientists searched for typologies of the accusing parent, child and the accused parent. They found that,

"Some of the false accusers were so obsessed with anger toward their estranged spouses that this became a major focus of their lives. They continued to be obsessed with abuse despite negative findings by mental health professionals and the courts, similar to what is found in cases of delusional disorder and Munchausen Syndrome by Proxy. The relationship of falsely accusing parents with their children was often characterized in the record as extremely controlling and symbiotic. Two [cases in their study] were given a formal diagnosis of *folie a deux* [folie a deux is when two people have the identical delusion—believing something is true which clearly could not be…sometimes called a shared psychotic disorder. Two individuals who plan and commit crimes that neither would concoct on their own. This unusual disorder is more likely to occur in a closely related pair…in French it means "shared madness [18]."] Several exhibited extremely serious dysfunction, such as unpredictable bizarre behavior, belief that they possessed supernatural powers and delusions of grandeur. These authors found more similarities than differences between mothers and fathers who falsely accused, with mothers very much in the majority [19, 5, 6]."

Mother's Delusional Disorder

In another study, the first stages of the mother's delusional disorder were present to some degree during the marriage and exacerbated parental conflicts prior to the separation. However, these subtle signs were not immediately discernible as a psychiatric illness and were only recognized in retrospect, as the mother's symptoms became worse in the course of the divorce and its associated disputes [20, 5, 6, 16].

EIGHTEEN

Parent Alienation Syndrome

"Any attempt at alienating the children from the other parent should be seen as a direct and willful violation of one of the prime duties of parenthood."
~Dr. J. Michael Bone (psychologist) and Michael R. Walsh (attorney), *Parental Alienation Syndrome: How to Detect It and What to Do About It*

Nearly three years before I began to write this book, childhood friends of mine—who were high school sweethearts and still married—visited our farm in Kentucky for a long weekend. They are the type of friends who genuinely want to know what's going on and who understand our situation, so I was able to process with them differences in approach to children in parents who have been alienated versus those that have never experienced alienation.

> Me: *"No, Steven has not had contact with his sons, and yes, one is now eighteen."*
> Friend: *"They will figure it out eventually and be back in his life."*

Instead of becoming offended I realized that they, of course, recognized this as the normal and typical response of someone who has been able to freely communicate with his children and had his relationship with them encouraged and supported by his wife. It is incomprehensible that the parent-child bond could ever be broken, and the parent not always be open to the child.

Questioning about our alienated children is the single most hurtful and misunderstood part of our story to date. Well-meaning people quickly advise that "they will figure it out and come back around." "Blood is blood, you can't change that." "Just make sure you keep telling them you will always love them." When this unsolicited advice is given, I shut down immediately and change the subject. How do others know so confidently that everything will be fine and that alienated children will come around? The next section explains PAS and the depth of the damage—likely irreversible.

Baker and Fine, in their book *Surviving Parent Alienation: A Journey of Hope and Healing* find that, about 20% of divorces are considered high conflict. This means there are frequent court visits, allegations of abuse and chronic disagreements in regard to parenting schedules. One parent becomes the favored parent and the other, the target parent. The targeted parent loses time with his or her children and they, in turn, become distant and cruel. The target parent does not know when or if their children will come back to them [21]. PAS children not only lose a parent, they lose siblings, cousins, aunts, uncles and grandparents. They not only grieve the death-like loss of these relationships, they mourn alone, not wanting to upset the alienating parent. Often, even the child's good memories of the target parent are lost and history is re-written with brainwashing techniques.

According to J. Michael Bone and Michael R. Walsh, PAS is becoming a more familiar term, but there is still a great deal of confusion around its detection. They point out that the phenomenon of one parent turning the child against the other parent is not a complicated concept, but historically it has been difficult to identify clearly [22].

In their 1999 seminal study they describe four very specific criteria that can be used to identify potential PAS. "The criteria described below are fairly easy to identify, separate and apart from the court file. When there is uncertainty about any of them, these criteria can be used to guide the attorney in the deposing of witnesses as well as in their examination in court [22]."

Steven and I have put together documentation that he sent to his attorney, along with emails that Jo sent to Steven in order to provide evidence of her meeting these criteria, as the alienating parent, though it took years for it to finally be realized and it is too late to be reconciled.

Criteria I: Access and Contact Blocking

> "Criteria I involves the active blocking of access or contact between the child and the absent parent...One of the most common [forms] is that of protection...the absent parent's parental judgment is inferior and, therefore, the child is much worse off from the visit. In extreme cases, this will take the form of allegations of child abuse, quite often sexual abuse...On a more subtle and common level, an argument heard for the blocking of visitation is that seeing the absent parent is "unsettling" to the child, and that they need time "to adjust." The message here is that the absent parent is treated less like a key family member and more like an annoying acquaintance that the child must see at times. Over time, this pattern can have a seriously erosive effect on the child's relationship with the absent parent. An even more subtle expression of this is that the visitation is "inconvenient," thereby relegating it to the status of an errand or chore. Again, the result is the erosion of the relationship between the child and the

absent or "target" parent...The common thread to all of these tactics is that one parent is superior and the other is not and, therefore, should be peripheral to the child's life. The alienating parent in these circumstances is acting inappropriately as a gatekeeper for the child to see the absent parent. When this occurs for periods of substantial time, the child is given the unspoken but clear message that one parent is senior to the other...The important concept here is that each parent is given the responsibility to promote a positive relationship with the other parent [22]."

Here is an example of Jo preventing contact (Steven provided to his attorney):

Dates	Call Attempts	Calls Answered or Returned
4/7-5/6 2012	16	03
3/7-4/6 2012	16	02
2/7-3/6 2012	14	02
1/7-2/6 2012	15	02
12/7-1/6 2012	With Steven	
11/7-12/6 2011	22	03
10/7-11/6 2011	17	03
9/7-10/6 20111	09	02
8/7-9/6 2011	23	07
7/7-8/6 2011	23	07
6/6-7/7/2011	Summer Visit with Steven	
TOTAL	178	36

After Steven finally had regular Skype sessions ordered in 2012, for most of that year, each boy would come on screen and say, "I have nothing to say to you," and then the other would appear and say, "I have nothing to say to you," and then Skype would abruptly end.

Email 10/16/2011

"Even when a schedule is given to you, you do not respect it. But I do tell them that you call and I tell them to call you back. It is in their right whether

they wish to return your phone calls or not, without a fight. And under the circumstances, one might think you need to give them some time and respect their feelings."

Email 3/20/2012

"Steven, we will need to discuss this further. We need to work on these dates together and consider the kids as well. This was the order by the judge to work together. Not including the kids in the planning is not fair to them…"

Email 3/27/2012

"I did not plan for the boys to have activities during your visitation, however, they are finishing up school and sports at the end of May. Unfortunately, you have not taken that into consideration in planning their trip nor did you confer with me before booking the flights. You are supposed to be contacting me so we can work out the dates together. The day you become more understanding of the kids and their feelings, the smoother things will work."

Email 9/6/2012

"Thank goodness they have a mom like me, in which I continue to stress their father's love, aside from the difficulties that continually arise." "Plus from a moral and an ethical stand point, I would imagine somethings need to be brought to your awareness. (1) The boys never like traveling on the day they get out of school, which also equals evening travel and usually not the best idea for the boys. (2) I would like you to think about how this trip might make the kids feel. I know on recent trips, they have been tricked and deceived. Once again, the boys will be thrown into a situation they have no control of or were lied/ tricked into. I could give examples, but I'm sure you know very well every visitation has been like that for them. They are expressing a great deal of uneasiness about this trip. Think about them and how they are going to feel, seeing you haven't told them what they are truly in for, and yet again, having no say, forced into a strange environment with strangers no less, automatically wanting them to except as family. Just think about it. Give them time, only forcing them will strain your relationship. They really would just like to be with you, not doing your errand work. And for number (3) and certainly the most alarming is the boys safety…"

Email 12/30/2012

"Clearly your inablility to see what has been plainly bothering the boys is troubling. And you feeling that making up stories and spouting lies to cast the blame on someone else is also very troubling. Mark Twain once said, "If you tell the truth, you don't have to remember anything." Unfortunately, that is not the case with you, as your stories get more far fetched and I have to present documentation that states otherwise... As for you, Steven, questioning the nature of my parenting skills, I have always taken excellent care of both boys. They are amazing boys who are well rounded and well adjusted, even in the midst of your shenanigans. I am constantly providing a positive atmosphere full of love, family and friends. They are thriving, growing young men who would't be that way if it weren't for myself and the love of my parents...

...And as a parent, a very good parent at that, I exercised that discretion. It was either let the boys breathe and recover for the next Skype session, or let them carry that bitterness to the next time and so on."

Criteria II: Unfounded Abuse Allegations

"The second criteria is related to false or unfounded accusations of abuse against the absent parent. The most strident expression of this is the false accusation of sexual abuse. It has been well studied that the incident of false allegations of sexual abuse account for over half of those reported, when the parents are divorcing or are in conflict over some post dissolution issue.... When the record shows that even one report of such abuse is ruled as unfounded, the interviewer is well advised to look for other expressions of false accusations [22]."

Email 12/30/2012

"Then I was told at random Sabrina's abuse of her two older children. Then I was made aware of some activity that Sabrina told my sister of during a visit to my sister's so the boys could see their cousins. Sabrina mentioned things like: her son sleeping in a closet, her daughters hating her, her gay lifestyle, and so on...quite alarming.

Because I have had quite an interesting experience recently seeing that Sabrina is being investigated through social services making you, Steve, apparently under the watchful eye as well. I hope to get to the bottom of this of course. Maybe you both could help with that. I am also quite aware of other multiple offenses."

"Other examples of this might be found in allegations of physical abuse that investigators later rule as being unfounded. Interestingly our experience has been that there are fewer false allegations of physical abuse than of other forms of abuse, presumably because physical abuse leaves visible evidence. It is, of course, much easier to falsely accuse someone of something that leaves no physical sign and has no third-party witnesses [22]."

Email 12/30/12
"Oh the stories...I was told nothing good but only of concern; kids being locked up in a hotel room, boys finding wine bottles tucked under tables, Ms. Sabrina screaming at her ex-husband during her son's drop off. It's incredible what both boys have been subjected to during their stays with Steven."

"A much more common expression of this pattern would be that of what would be termed emotional abuse. When false allegations of emotional abuse are leveled, one often finds that what is present is actually differing parental judgment that is being framed as "abusive" by the absent parent...Or one parent might introduce a new "significant other" to the child before the other parent believes that they should and this might also be called "abusive" to the child [22]."

Email 12/3/2012
"It has been most alarming to see all the shenanigans and the great lengths you and your girlfriend have done to coverup or hide things. I have taken notice and more so I have taken notice to some alarming things the boys have brought to my attention on their own. I will need documentation from you and I'm sure other sources in the assurance of the boys safety.

Now, I will need some proper documentation on her drinking in front of her son or as I imagine her not being able to consume alcohol in front of her son and some signed assurances through the court that the both of you will not be drinking at anytime while the boys are in your care. We can go through the judge if you'd like or we can have our attorneys write something up accordingly, which ever you wish. I am sure this will be done hastily, because we have more pressing issues to take care of after this one.

Jo"

Email 12/13/11

"*They are uncomfortable with you doing this and don't want to share their time with you between another kid and a girlfriend. Steve, there is only so much I can do on this end, but I think you should be getting their input on how they feel and the way they want to spend their time with you. The way you left things with Thomas a couple weeks ago, he was sobbing uncontrollably with a couple of conversations you had with him because you weren't listening to him. They are afraid to tell you their feelings. I think we can work together on the issues with the kids. You have only a little over 2 weeks with them and springing this on them was not quite the best idea. I can't tell you what you should do but this subject has been weighing heavy on their mind since coming home from Alaska. Please put yourself in Thomas and Jay's shoes when you talk about Junior and Sabrina. They see you building a whole other life and doing things with them that you had years to do with the boys and didn't. In there minds you are very contradicting to the things you have said to them in the past. I'm really sorry, but I don't want this to hurt them or back fire on you. They don't see you much, so they don't want to deal with all the heavy stuff. They both want to go up to Michigan and spend time with you, you're your family..."*

Email 12/30/12

"*Or maybe it's Steve having his girlfriend out this past summer without telling the boys, They explicitly told you that they did not want to go to Kentucky to see your girlfriend, Sabrina, and they didn't want to see her period. You dismissed their feelings by telling them that you would talk about it when they got to Michigan. Then low and behold she shows up with her son (1 of 3 children, 2 daughters of which are not on speaking terms) right as the boys get to Michigan, giving them quite a shocking surprise. Then you proceed to take them to Kentucky without telling them or telling me, hiding their phones so they couldn't get help...*

...Or maybe it was when you bribed them to cut their hair and Sabrina shaved their heads with a dull razor, making them look like kids in a jewish concentration camp. (It took Jay weeks to recover and the hair dresser couldn't believe the damage that was done to both boys hair.) Or maybe it was Sabrina mentioning vulgar, inappropriate things to the boys in reference to movies, her gay parties, experiences with other woman. Or maybe it was the boxes of wine she drank....... not sure, but I'm willing to bet it was all of these things the boys have mention over time on their own.

...Addressing your fiance and the boys desire to talk to just you, is a reasonable request under the circumstances. It certainly is appropriate for the limited and most deceptive time that they have been forced or tricked into seeing her. Once again, it comes from a culmination of things that have been presented to them and they have verbally expressed to me on their own...

...Now, Thomas, on the other hand, was upset and visibly shaken and angry, verbally expressing how terrified he was for what the consequences might be from Steve of Thomas standing up to him [to not have me involved in communication with Steven]."

"When this phenomenon occurs in literally thousands of different ways and times, each of which seems insignificant on its own, the emotional atmosphere that it creates carries a clearly alienating effect on the child...the criteria is clearly present and identifiable when the parent is eager to hurl abuse allegations, rather than being cautious, careful and even reluctant to do so. This latter stance is more in keeping with the parent's responsibility to encourage and affirmatively support a relationship with the other parent...<u>Simply put, the responsible parent will give the other parent the benefit of the doubt... whereas the alienating parent will not miss an opportunity to accuse the other parent</u> [22]."

Email 12/30/12

"This is not the first time I have had to calm him down from this afraid state. This seems to be a constant go around with his dad for quite some time. It is not a great pleasure of mine to have to explain that nothing is going to happen to him and that he is safe....I have heard a mouthful from both boys over the years and even dating back to when we were parenting under the same

roof, Steven. You know this, because we have had numerous conversations on this; the kids being scared of you, their bitterness, sadness and so forth."

Criteria III: Deterioration in Relationship Since Separation

"The third of the criteria necessary for the detection of PAS is probably the least described or identified, but critically is one of the most important. It has to do with the existence of a positive relationship between the minor children and the now absent or nonresidential parent, prior to the marital separation; and a substantial deterioration, of it since then. Such a recognized decline does not occur on its own. It is, therefore, one of the most important indicators of the presence of alienation as well…as a full measure of its relative "success." …If this father is clearly trying to maintain a positive relationship with the children through observance of visitation and other activities and the children do not want to see him or have him involved in their lives, then one can only speculate that an alienation process may have been in operation. Children do not naturally lose interest in and become distant from their nonresidential parent simply by virtue of the absence of that parent. Also, healthy and established parental relationships do not erode naturally of their own accord. They must be attacked. Therefore, any dramatic change in this area is virtually always an indicator of an alienation process…the court can be easily swayed into premature closure or fooled into thinking that the turmoil of the separation environment is representative of the true parent-child relationship. Once this ruling is made by the court, it is an exacting challenge to correct its perception [22]."

The following is a school project written by Thomas five months before Steven gave Jo marriage dissolution papers. It is exactly as it appears on a school paper of which Steven took a photo. There is no problem between Steven and Thomas; on the contrary, Thomas seems to have a great deal of respect for Steven, as he should.

> **My Role Model**
> **My Dad**
> 9/14/09
>
> My role model is my Dad. First, he is a great Navy seal. Second, he's a great fisherman. Last, he's an awesome hunter. All in all, my Dad is a great Dad.
>
> My Dad is a great hunter! First, he's very calm. Whenever he finds an animal, he doesn't jump and get all excited. Also, he's very fast. I bed he could beat me running a mile! Finally, he has great accuracy. He's shot targets from 1,130 feet away! It turns out my Dad is an awesome hunter!
>
> My Dad is an amazing fisherman! First, he steps lightly and slowly on the rocks. He's so quiet I bet I can't see him coming! Second, I got all my tips from him. He says, "You have to make them angry to make them bite!" He also catches most of the fish! When we where fishing, he caught ten fish on his own! Rightfully so, my Dad is the best fisherman in the world!
>
> My Dad is a great Navy Seal. First of all, he's a Senior Chief in Virginia and here he teaches the B.U.D (basic underwater demolition) students. He takes the students to Long Island for training. Also, he used to deploy in Afghanistan. He went around fighting terrorists. Finally, he has three Bronze Stars and one Silver Star! The Bronze Stars are for his bravery in combat and the Silver Star is for him taking down and enemy plane regardless of his safety. It turns out my Dad is awesome at his job and is very courageous.
>
> My Dad is my role model! He is a talented Navy Seal! Also, he's a great fisher. Last, he's a talented hunter. My Dad is an awesome role model.

After Steven asked Jo for a divorce, and Jo made a false domestic violence accusation Steven was living in the barracks, where the students stay, at the command; he had no contact with the boys for more than a month. During this time, both boys wrote very disparaging letters about Steven. These letters and the unsubstantiated domestic violence accusation were central in Steven's loss of custody to Jo. This is Thomas's letter that Steven's attorney gave to him just prior to the divorce trial:

> Dear Daddy,
>
> Daddy, you come home drunk sometimes and get drunk at home. I scares Jay and I. A lot of times you come home and hurt mom after drinking. It makes me really mad. I watched you nearly drop Jay on the concrete at the Hilton back in Virginia. You scared Jay and I when you were trying to say goodnight after the Sushi party at K's house.
>
> I got pretty mad when you hurt mom. I tried to hold the door shut when you were chasing mom up the stairs. I did that because I wanted to protect her. I heard you hit mom, and it was loud. I hear you yell at mom when you guys were going down the stairs saying, "are you going to tell everyone I beat you up?" I was thinking I needed to go downstairs and help mom. I was angry that you put mom in physical therapy. (How can you hurt people you love) I saw mom hurt really bad afterwards.
>
> This trip we took to come here made me upset and very angry because you haven't kept any of your promises. You promised that we would help plan the trip and we didn't. We kind of liked some of these things, but we didn't decide on any of it. You kept saying we couldn't stay in a hotel because we didn't have enough money or we didn't make the money. We heard that the whole trip. You said that all the time. You said that we would be able to visit our friends in Virginia while we were here, but then you said we wouldn't until we move back. I cried, you were fighting with me about it. You didn't understand, you didn't care. You said I could always tell you how I feel, but I couldn't because you scare me, or wouldn't hear what I say or you will get angry. You said we moved to Kodiak to be a family and spend more time with each other, but it was pretty much the same as Virginia Beach, but much worse. You said we could get to help choose a home but that didn't happen. I never felt like this was our home. I felt like it was your home, not ours.
>
> I'm angry and a little disappointed, and scared you hurting everybody. I miss seeing you, the nicer you. I love you.
>
> Sincerely Thomas
>
> P.S. I can't wait to see you again

Hands down this is a very damning letter. It's easy to see how this document could raise questions and concerns about Steven to those not familiar with PAS and especially when he had nothing to counter the content, only his word. If this letter is taken into context with some other critical pieces, it loses its effect and raises questions in the other direction. Thomas is ten years old writing a letter about protecting his mother; if the father was that angry and violent ("I heard you hit mom, and it was loud") and the violence had been chronic ("*a lot* of times you come home and hurt mom after drinking") that child would likely be very afraid and hide/huddle with his younger brother; he would not get in the middle of a violent conflict or move toward the violent conflict. In reality, the boys were annoyed at the interaction between Jo and Steven; they asked them to leave because they were interrupting their video game. The last paragraphs concern adult issues. A ten-year-old boy would NOT be concerned about the planning of a trip with his "dad the role model" to Alaska, nor the activities that did or did not happen. A ten-year-old boy would never care enough about helping to buy a house that he would put it in a letter to his role model dad after his dad had just moved out.

Steven's domestic violence accusation was not investigated so it never went to the level of a substantiated or unsubstantiated ruling of domestic violence, following an investigation. If Jo had demanded injuries into the bruises/markings, the police would've taken photos. These photos would've been presented as evidence in court both then and at the divorce trial. There were no pictures. Additionally, why weren't there police interview reports corroborating statements made in the boys' letters submitted, as evidence, to the court in the divorce?

Jo went to the emergency room at some point after the false accusation. Medical professionals are "mandatory reporters" meaning that they must report, to social services and/or law enforcement, if any sort of abuse is suspected. Neither agency was called about Jo's chief complaints, originating from an alleged domestic violence incident, when in the emergency room, lending credence to this being a false claim.

Further, when Steven appeared in court a few weeks later and was asked about the incident he said, "I had given her marriage dissolution papers right before I left for a trip and when I got home, she made this accusation." The case was dismissed. A family court judge, more than a year after the accusation, with no police report or emergency room report, made a ruling of domestic violence, which countered local law enforcement and medical professional decisions in this case.

Court professionals bear great responsibility in the examination of pre- and post-relationships, if they don't, then they become part of the PA process.

Criteria IV: Intense Fear Reaction by Children

"The fourth criteria necessary for the detection of PAS is admittedly more psychological than the first three. It refers to an obvious fear reaction on the part of the children, of displeasing or disagreeing with the potentially alienating parent in regard to the absent or potential target parent. Simply put, an alienating parent operates by the adage, "My way or the highway." If the children disobey this directive, especially in expressing positive approval of the absent parent, the consequences can be very serious…The child, in effect, is put into a position of being the alienating parent's "agent" and is continually being put through various loyalty tests. The important issue here is that the alienating parent thus forces the child to choose parents. This, of course, is in direct opposition to a child's emotional well-being...When the child does dare to defy the alienating parent, they quickly learn that there is a serious price to pay. Consequently, children who live such lives develop an acute sense of vigilance over displeasing the alienating parent...these children learn to manipulate just to survive...telling partial truths, and then telling out-and-out lies...Given this understanding, it is perhaps easier to see why children, in an effort to cope with this situation, often find it easier if they begin to internalize the alienating parent's perceptions of the absent parent and begin to echo these feelings. This is one of the most compelling and dramatic effects of PAS, that is, hearing a child vilifying the absent parent and joining the alienating parent in such attacks...This, of course, is compounded when the expert is also not sensitive to this powerful fear component, and believes that the child is voicing his or her own inner feelings in endorsing the "no visitation" plan (23)."

Jo started immediately with the boys' letters to Steven, explained in the previous criteria. The consequence of this "intense fear reaction" manifests in the boys when they become teenagers; this is detailed later.

NINETEEN

The Psychological Effects of PAS on the Alienated Parent

"Your beloved child is being taken from you, and no one understands. No one helps."
~Dr. Craig Childress

"Focus, understandably, has been on the best interest of the child regarding custody and resulting deprivation of a parent due to "abuses," but there is very little about the traumatic effects on the parent experiencing the unnecessary loss of their child(ren). In my experience, it is nothing less than grieving a death—one does not know if they will ever see their child(ren) again and happy memories and sacrifices for the child are lost in cruelty and misunderstanding [23]."

Dr. Childress goes beyond the current scope of PAS research, by addressing the actions of the perpetrating parent and their devastating effects on the alienated parent. He has developed a model: Attachment Based Parent Alienation (AB-PA).

"The trauma experienced by the custodial parent is re-enacted in the current family structure—the parent is still the abused child seeking atonement for the wrongs inflicted upon them. The three parts necessary for the manifestation of this model are a "victimized child," an "abusive parent," and a "protective parent." The trauma reenactment narrative requires the child(ren) to accept the role as "victimized child." Once that is accepted, there must be a perpetrator [23]."

The letters that the children wrote when Steven was out of the house were a critical turning point; they became convinced that they and their mother were the victims of Steven's abuse—he was the monster. This automatically imposed onto him the role of "abusive parent."

"The targeted parent is immediately put on the defensive, and must continually try to prove to therapists and others that he or she is not "abusive" of the child. It doesn't matter that the parenting practices of the targeted parent are entirely normal-range. The moment the child is induced by the distorted parenting practices of the narcissistic/(borderline) parent into adopting the "victimized child's role in the trauma reenactment narrative, the "abusive parent" role is immediately imposed upon the targeted parent…The child's acceptance of the "victimized child" role also invites and provides the context for the narcissistic/(borderline) parent to adopt and conspicuously display to the child and to others the coveted role as the all-wonderful, perfect and idealized, "protective parent."

…These two roles in the trauma reenactment narrative are mutually supporting. The emotional and psychological trauma and profound grief of attachment-based "parental alienation" consumes the life and psychology of the targeted parent…The difficult and challenging relationship with the hostile-rejecting child; the chaos of trying to work with the narcissistic/(borderline) parent to schedule visitations; the blatant and repeated disregard of court orders by the narcissistic/(borderline) parent; and the continual intrusions and disruptions by the narcissistic/(borderline) parent into the relationship of the targeted parent with the child, continually consume the focus of the targeted parent…

Repeated court dates, lawyers, therapists, custody evaluations, that all occur in the context of continuing parent-child conflict, act to fully captivate the complete psychological involvement of the targeted parent…And in this upside-down world, the targeted parent is continually being blamed for the child's rejection, even though the targeted parent did nothing wrong…

But none of this false drama is true. It is delusional. The parenting of the targeted parent is entirely normal range, and the child is in no danger and doesn't need any "protection." It is a false narrative born in the childhood relationship trauma of the narcissistic/(borderline) parent [23]."

TWENTY

Cut Him in Half

"O my lord, give her the living child, and by no means kill him!" But the other said, "Let him be neither mine nor yours, but divide him." So, the king answered and said, "Give the first woman the living child, and by no means kill him; she is his mother." And all Israel heard of the judgment which the king had rendered; and they feared the king, for they saw that the wisdom of God was in him to administer justice.

~1 Kings 3:26-28, New King James Version

I encountered Dr. Childress's research for the first time in 2018 while working on this book. Years prior, I unknowingly made this critical connection by observing Jo and by learning from Steven what she had revealed to him about her past. I had a feeling that she had been abused. After she found out about me, Steven and I would pay for every person that had ever hurt her. Following Steven's hearing, in 2013, for a Protective Order when the judge suggested that he find "relief" through family court, Steven and I provided information to his attorney in support of a motion asking for relief from Jo's abusive behavior toward us.

> "I think it is in the boy's best interest to make the court aware of some delicate information that I believe has an impact on Jo's parenting, interactions with me and other adults, and her overall mental health. Jo suffered a traumatic brain injury during college in a vehicle accident. The car crash caused severe head trauma. Jo said she experienced such intense migraines, as a result of the crash, that she would go blind. She would remain in bed for the entire day. She could not possibly be available to the boys during these times and I wonder who is caring for the boys during these frequent episodes. Jo has told me, and most of my family, of her father's on-going sexual, mental and physical abuse, detailing the abuse to me a number of times. Jo has said that her father was and still is an alcoholic. I have only seen her father during two occasions. The first was our wedding. The second was when she went to his house with the boys during a Christmas we spent in Michigan. We spent 15-20 minutes there. She wanted <u>me</u> to go to <u>protect her and the boys</u>. I believe Jo has twisted the abuse she experienced at the hands of her father, in her childhood, onto me. I believe that is why she is able to paint me so well as a monster. I believe she is coercing my boys to tell stories that in reality happened to her and reliving her childhood trauma saying my boys have suffered in ways she has, but not what has really happened between my boys and myself. Stories I've heard from Jo's childhood bear a striking resemblance to the false accusations Jo has made about me."

TWENTY-ONE

The Female Sociopath

Dr. Childless describes the alienating parent as having the personality disorder of "narcissistic/borderline." Borderline personality disorder (BPD) could explain Jo's polarized view of Steven and of their relationship: idealization "all is good" and devaluation "all is bad." Steven picked up this dichotomy, but the fact that her mood swings were dependent upon intense personal relationships and an intense fear of abandonment does not suggest a bi-polar disorder. Her desire to accelerate intimacy and to secure a love attachment using threats is textbook BPD, and her mirroring Steven's interests and passions is another red flag. At times, Jo resembles Alex Forrest —Glen Close's classic cinematic portrayal of BPD in *Fatal Attraction* —it was impossible for her mind to accept that her relationship with Steven was really over, as evidenced by her threats to make everything "right" if he just came back to her. If she simply kept doing things—keeping him engaged in any way—eventually he would come back. She didn't care on what terms their interaction occurred, just that he responded, that he did not ignore her.

The female BPD and the male Sociopath dance very close to one another. They both feed off of the actions—or perceived actions—of someone else, though in different ways; the nature of these disorders generally requires another person. The BPD individual clings to a person of attachment while acting, both inwardly and outwardly, often destructively, from a place of hurt. They are unable to control emotional responses or reconcile what has happened in the past with how to live in the present. The sociopath acts out from a place of entitlement and superiority, without necessarily having a history of abuse. The major difference between these two profiles is that a person suffering from BPD can, and likely does, feel great shame after an episode of an uncontrolled emotional response; they often want to get better. A sociopath, on the other hand, does not feel shame or remorse and does not recognize that they have done anything wrong—someone else is always to blame.

While Jo exhibits some BPD characteristics, in my professional and personal opinion, she is a sociopath. Jo's actions are similar to Peter's actions with slight differences in execution; they are the same in their fearless abuse of institutional systems to their own benefit, and in that they have no consideration for rules or laws, and cannot negotiate. Neither one can be reasoned with; they are not wrong—they know best and they are the victim 100% of the time. Most importantly, they show no signs of remorse or empathy toward even their own children. *Sociopathy is essential to successfully carry out PAS with full alienation.* Severe PAS, as in both of Steven's case and my own, is the worst psychologically abusive act that a parent can inflict upon their child for two reasons 1) the parent-child relationship is the ultimate power imbalance and 2) a parent is in collusion with their own child and they coerce this child to destroy someone who has offered to them love and security. The alienated parent has always been a significant part of the child's life—not only do they lose this relationship they must also hate the parent and act accordingly.

> *"According to the American Psychiatric Association's Diagnostic and Statistical Manual of Mental Disorders V, antisocial personality disorder [Sociopathy] includes 1) ego-centrism derived from personal gain, power or pleasure; 2) impairments in interpersonal functioning including, a) lack of empathy, concern for feelings, needs or suffering of others, lack of remorse after hurting or mistreating another, and b) incapacity for intimacy or mutually intimate*

relationships, as exploitation is a primary means of relating to others, including by deceit or coercion and use of dominance or intimidation to control others; 3) antagonism using, a) manipulativeness to influence or control others, use of seduction, charm, glibness to achieve one's ends, b) deceitfulness by dishonesty and fraudulence, a misrepresentation of self, embellishment or fabrication when relating events, c) callousness or a lack of concern for feelings or problems of others, lack of guilt or remorse about the negative or harmful effects of one's actions on others, d) hostility with persistent or frequent angry feelings, irritability in response to minor slights and insults, mean, nasty, or vengeful behavior; and 4) disinhibition by, a) irresponsibility or disregard for and failure to honor financial and other obligations or commitments, lack of respect for and lack of follow through on agreements d) hostility with persistent or frequent angry feelings, irritability in response to minor slights and insults, mean, nasty, or vengeful behavior; and 4) disinhibition by, a) irresponsibility or disregard for and failure to honor financial and other obligations or commitments, lack of respect for and lack of follow through on agreements and promises, b) impulsivity or acting on the spur of the moment in response to immediate stimuli, acting on a momentary basis with-out a plan or considering outcomes, and difficulty establishing and following plans [24].

According to the book *The Sociopath Next Door* by Martha Stout, one type of sociopath is the non-ambitious type [25].

"You are the sort of person who really does not want much of anything. Your only real ambition is not to have to exert yourself to get by. You do not want to work like everyone else does… Without a conscience, you can nap or pursue your hobbies, or watch television, or just hang out somewhere all day long… Living a bit on the fringes, and with handouts from relatives and friends, you can do this indefinitely. People may whisper to one another that you are an underachiever, or that you are depressed, a sad case, or in contrast, if they get angry, they may grumble that you are lazy…A partner does not have to be rich, just a financier that is reliably conscience bound [25]."

What better occupation for a sociopath's spouse than the military? It carries consistent and steadily increasing pay—(Special Operators (Spec Ops) receive additional pay. Steven received jump pay, dive pay, demolition pay and hazardous duty pay, and his re-enlistment bonuses were substantially higher than non-Spec Ops. He also enjoyed a retirement package, special privileges on bases, Servicemen's Group Life Insurance (SGLI), medical, dental and prescription insurance, Commissary and Exchange, Morale Welfare and Recreation, spouse educational programs and employment placement and the post 911 GI Bill.

Most importantly, if the marriage lasts until the ten-year mark, the financial formula changes significantly. Jo will receive one-third of Steven's retirement for the rest of her life or until he dies. If he dies before she does, she will receive the survival death benefit. Reading through hundreds of pages of Jo's emails in preparation for this book, I am amazed at how much she knows about the overall benefits.

I am not diminishing the gravity of the cases in which soldiers are genuinely abusive to their spouses, and the victim is not believed because of important rank or military influence. In my work with domestic violence data, I, of course, encounter cases in which a soldier returns from combat and becomes abusive or escalates abuse.

I thought that I had come up with a novel hypothesis that a sociopath would seek out a spouse in the military when I came across the term: Dependapotamus. Granted, I found it in the Urban Dictionary—not a typical source for a researcher—however, it does give credence to the concept because it has happened to enough military personnel that the cumulative effect has been to name and define it.

According to Urban Dictionary,
"*A Dependapotamus is the spouse of a military service member, whose*

symbiotic relationship is parasitic. These creatures seek to take advantage of the trusting nature of the more inexperienced service member by [bearing] children to him, to establish a link that would be more work to be rid of than to simply keep. Often times, by bearing multiple children, the desire to flee from the parasitic clutches of the Dependapotamus....the service member is reduced to such a low that the service member simply settles for his/her misfortune, and does not leave. Typical behavior is to sit at home, as they do not work...talk on the phone to other Dependapotami, while ignoring the children to whom she serves as 'caregiver.' ...Often, they sell the idea of not working or pursuing education...claiming to 'stay at home with the kids.'...They are dramatic, loud, immature, obnoxious, freeloading, belligerent, unfaithful (when applicable, most are too unattractive to cheat), gossiping, wasteful, hateful, bigamous and click-y [26]."

Jo was able to "fake it" somewhat during the two-week periods when Steven was stateside on leave because they generally used these times to travel to visit family. As a result, they didn't have many established routines or much time together as a couple. Steven says that at the start of his time at home, Jo cooked and cleaned and was engaged, but by the time he was ready to leave, the laundry was piled and dirty dishes filled the sink, while she would sleep more and more.

Their trip to move to Alaska was the longest period of time that Jo and Steven had spent alone together. During the trip—once in Michigan at the start of the trip, and then again in Idaho—Jo threatened to return to Virginia Beach with the children while Steven took an unaccompanied tour in Alaska. She claimed that she wanted Steven to be home more and for him to spend more time with the boys; he had taken the billet in order to do just that. It had become clear to him that, ultimately, she didn't want a marriage; she wanted the perks of his career and to control his life as well as the lives of their children. It often occurred to him that she would prefer to be a Navy SEAL widow so that she would have complete control of their story, his money and benefits, and their children's lives.

Navy SEAL's wives hold prestigious standing, both in the military and the civilian communities, and Jo used this authority to belittle other military and civilian wives. When I moved into the Virginia Beach home where Jo had lived, neighbors relayed to me stories of how Jo elevated herself and presented as superior because of Steven's position and successes. She had been so cruel to many of her former friends and neighbors about their husbands, and then contradicted herself by disparaging Steven; these people found it a relief to vent to me. Though the information about Jo was entirely negative, the conversations took their toll and I found myself being controlled emotionally by this woman.

TWENTY-TWO

Jo and Peter Join Forces: The Creepers

"The likelihood that a mother or a father will become the target parent in an alienation scenario increases according to who is seen as responsible for the marital break-up. The risk increases when the parent seen as responsible for the break-up is discovered to have actually been unfaithful or become involved with a new partner immediately after the separation."
~Dr. Richard Gardner, *Recent Trends in Divorce and Custody Litigation*

It's good and bad that both Steven and I were both married to nearly identical individuals. It's good because we believe one another, without hesitation, and we take any communication from one another's ex-spouses very seriously. Steven helps me respond to my situation and I help him with his. It's bad because it doubles the stress for both of us. We are rarely free from attacks from at least one of our exes.

Jo's communication is often irrational and emotional, though very resolute in her schemes to destroy Steven for leaving her; whereas Peter is a dangerously intelligent manipulator. She is very direct in her parent alienation while undermining the children's respect for Steven; Peter is more insidious and undetectable. Both achieve the same results. Together, they fill us with more trepidation than either of them could on their own.

Steven and I share with one another all communications from these two individuals. In a late 2012 email, Jo made a statement that made both Steven and I think she and Peter were in communication. During Christmas break in 2012, while I was with Steven in Alaska, he received from Jo an email that confirmed our suspicions. Her email mentioned a social services case that Peter initiated with me before he moved out of the country. Peter could not have known that the case was closed as unsubstantiated; only the accused is notified of the findings. Her misinformation about an ongoing social services case against me came from Peter. These records are confidential. She either received the information directly from Peter or he easily could have "convinced" my oldest daughter to communicate with Jo by inciting my daughter's anger toward and by framing Steven as the reason for the broken marriage. Regardless of the means, Peter and Jo were sharing information. That Christmas the same accusations that I fought in my own case began to appear in Steven's case.

Both Jo and Peter, very proudly, continued to send emails that included information that only the other one knew. They meant to unsettle Steven and me.

TWENTY-THREE

Spring Break 2012

"Children in alignments were found to be less psychologically healthy than those whose divorce adjustment allowed them to maintain their affection for both parents."
   ~Dr. J.S. Wallerstein and Dr. J.B. Kelly, Surviving the Breakup: How Children and Parents Cope with Divorce

Steven and I decided to get married in Myrtle Beach where my family lived at the time. I set up a photographer to take engagement and wedding photos. Steven had visitation with his boys for spring break and I had Junior—we were on the same custody arrangement schedule. Communications from both Peter and Jo indicated their wishes to prevent spring break visitation. Engaged, it was time to introduce his boys to my family, and we wanted to include all three of our boys in the engagement photos. My dad rented a very nice condo for us and we all looked forward to a fun vacation. Jo and Peter knew of our plans.

The boys flew into Myrtle Beach and we all went to my brother and sister-in-law's house. Little did I know—Steven knew—they had planned a huge engagement party alongside a welcome-to the-family party for Thomas and Jay. They rented a bouncy house and a bouncy water slide, decorated the house, had a huge food spread and an engagement cake. Thomas and Jay fit right in with Junior's cousins. Everyone got along very well. Jay immediately started calling my nieces and nephews cousins and Thomas started carrying my youngest niece around with him.

That evening, we overheard Jay on the phone with Jo. He excitedly told her how much fun he was having with his new cousins. He stopped and his expression changed from laughing to sad. After he got off of the phone, he said that he was not allowed to call my nieces and nephews cousins—he was told that they were not his family.

We had a very romantic engagement photo shoot and at the end included our boys in a few shots with us. Steven's boys had trouble taking it seriously and kept making faces and sexual gestures. I could see a pattern of them bringing chaos into otherwise happy and settled situations. My sister-in-law talked about this with me, she saw it too.

Steven's mother was also visiting and stayed with my parents—she wanted to spend time with Steven's boys, whom she hadn't seen for a while, and meet my family. They all got along well.

At the end of the week, Junior and I went back to Kentucky, Steven, to Alaska, and his boys, to Florida—it was a sad parting for everyone.

TWENTY-FOUR

The NCIS Investigation

A year into the divorce proceedings, Jo returned to Virginia. While Steven was away on deployments Jo was the sole representative of the family, so people were apt to believe her, initially.

Jo returned to her former community under the guise of reuniting with dear friends, but it was really an attempt to destroy Steven's career and his reputation (refer to the "neighbor's letter"). To this day, we don't know the whole story; the Naval Criminal Investigation Services (NCIS) investigator wouldn't tell Steven everything, just that his ex-wife claimed that Steven had secret information taken from a work laptop Steven shared with his entire sniper troop saved on a home computer. Jo claimed to be traumatized by what she found. Her allegations were so serious that they initiated a years-long NCIS investigation that could have led to a dishonorable discharge for Steven and others. She had to plot for years to secretly download and save information from his work laptop and/or his own personal laptop—which he sometimes used for work because of having to share only one work computer with many operators. In the end, it came out that this was a vindictive and jealous ex-wife, and that her claims were completely contrary to his character.

When I spoke with the investigator, as a personal character

witness, he said that everyone he had interviewed provided the same accolades about Steven as I had. All gathered information was consistent; if it had not been, things would not have gone well for Steven. Jo could have accomplished what she sought.

Additionally, Jo claimed that Steven had a private detective following her during her visit to Virginia, and that Steven stalked her. She made these accusations to superiors more senior than those in Alaska. After this visit, most of her friends in Virginia Beach refused to respond to any communication from her.

After more than a year of a full-blown NCIS investigation, Steven was interviewed. The timing of the accusation means that Jo set it in motion right around the time that Steven shared the marriage dissolution papers with her. She threatened him, and she likely returned to Virginia Beach in order to be interviewed. Steven's interview was his first knowledge of the investigation. His superiors were questioned without his knowledge; he was dangerously close to losing his career and honor. Realizing that he was up against breathtaking depths of intentional malice, he became suicidal. Steven was *deeply* affected; he was so overwhelmed that he found it difficult to maintain normal daily activities. He self-medicated with alcohol and became more irresponsible than he had ever before been. He didn't care anymore. Steven teetered between suicidal ideation and "practicing" the act of suicide with a firearm, with the intention to complete, several times.

According to Thomas Joiner's pioneering and internationally recognized *"Theory of Interpersonal-Psychological Suicidal Behavior,"* the desire for death is composed of two psychological states, one being, "Burdensomeness" and the other "Low Belonging/Social Alienation:" the experience that one is alienated from others, not an integral part of a family, circle of friends (Steven was the boss not "one of the guys"), or other valued group. Steven was thousands of miles from me, his children and any support system. He was continually facing threats that his children would be taken from him and he had little-to no support from his family. Those two psychological states, in combination with the ability to overcome the natural instinct for self-preservation can be a deadly combination. In Joiner's theory, suicide victims literally "work up" to the act by practicing. People often think that those who die by suicide are weak. You cannot do it unless you are fearless, and this behavior is learned [27, 28, 29].

The *"Acquired Ability to Enact Lethal Self-Injury"* can be developed from repeated exposure to painful or fearsome experiences which creates a higher tolerance for pain and a sense of fearlessness in the face of death—a capacity to stare down the self-preservation instinct [27, 28, 29]. The training and career of a U.S. Navy Seal.

The most current research in veteran suicide shows that combat-related issues with the additional stress of intimate partner problems (e.g., hostile divorces) put veterans at a high risk of suicide [30]. Involuntary Child Absence Syndrome is related to the stress reaction of some fathers, regardless of military service, due to involuntary separation from their children. A psychiatrist who studies divorce and fatherhood found that fathers may have an equally strong need to nurture and parent and feel profound loss and frustrations when their post-divorce relationships with their children are diminished, minimal or nonexistent. For veterans, losing children compounds combat-related injuries and heightens the risk of suicide. Steven's decision to take the Alaska position had everything to do with his desire to be much more involved in his boys' lives at a critical time in their development (2009, ages nine and six), knowing that at their ages they needed their father more than ever [31].

His world was falling apart. I called him nearly every hour to check on his wellbeing. I called his commanding officer and, without using the word "suicidal," I implied it and asked him to watch Steven closely. Within weeks he was sent to Virginia Beach as a hardship case.

Upon receiving marriage dissolution papers from Steven, Jo took three calculating actions: she filed a false domestic violence allegation, she initiated an NCIS investigation, and she had her sons (ten and seven) write crushing letters about their dad, also making false allegations. Any one of these three acts could have led to a dishonorable discharge from the Navy for Steven and that left him teetering dangerously close to suicide.

When Steven gave the completed paperwork to Jo, he assumed that they would move forward unmarried, while working together to raise the boys; she seemed just as miserable as he was in the marriage. He never anticipated her reaction. Never. Jo stayed true to her words, "This is not how it is going to happen."

TWENTY-FIVE

Steven's Brother, Ross, and Jo

When a toxic person can no longer control you, they will try to control how others see you. The misinformation will feel unfair, but stay above it, trusting that other people will eventually see the truth, just like you did.
  ~*Jill Blakeway*

Our experiences during our divorces amplified the fear that Steven and I felt. A highly decorated warrior who lived in fear of opening his email dreading what Jo would do next. He disabled email notification sounds so that he could be intentional about when and how often he subjected himself to her emotionally destructive communication; he could ready himself for an attack from Jo.

In 2012 we hid from confrontation, sometimes betraying ourselves and one another in an effort to not upset the balance, mistakenly thinking that we couldn't handle anything else. The process of divorcing Jo and Peter created the most difficult years, by far, in each of our lives—our darkest days. I choose to communicate the most damaging parts of our stories to show *how* we climbed out, despite the discomfort that it causes. We trust that our story will help others journey through similar tragedy with more grace. We are called to tell our stories so we can be interconnected with one another. If we don't relay our experiences, how can we find and comfort each other in this vast sometimes overwhelming world?

After Peter filed the first horrific motion leaving me utterly exposed and humiliated, I reached out to my family. I had been estranged for four years prior to this, and I was not behaving as the best daughter or sister. As they are apt to do, my family put hand in hand, surrounding me—the walls of a mighty fortress. I told my story and described what I was up against, but I did not have to convince them. This was a war, and I needed refuge somewhere. My support grew to include my extended family, along with long time friends of Peter Walton's family—and also my son's Godparents.

Peter stated, during a parent coordination meeting, that he couldn't believe that my brothers wouldn't talk to him; he had been friends with them nearly his whole life (when Peter and I met, his and my youngest brothers were both nine years old). The parent coordinator said that, in cases like this, it is completely normal for each family to take care of their own. I had that luxury; Steven did not.

When my family learned of Steven, he was the only partner that they acknowledged. They were thrilled that I finally had someone *good*, and that there was hope of a happy ending for me. My family adores Steven, and they all have a great deal of respect for him. Both nieces and nephews love their Uncle Steven; he is their hero.

I was introduced to Ross's wife, in May of 2011. By this time, Steven and Jo were officially divorced. Between this meeting in May and the Christmas described in "The Family that Stole Christmas (*I*

Married a Sociopath, Chapter 50)," Betsy did nothing short of campaign against me. Information from that first motion—the one that left me utterly exposed and humiliated—flowed from Peter to Jo, from Jo to Betsy, and from Betsy to the women in Steven's family. It was happening all over again...I endured the initial abuse, litigated it for a year, litigated it again in Steven's case, and now here it was again: re-victimized. I had already disputed everything that was untrue, legally and formally. I thought it was done. In hostile divorces, parties disclose the worst things about each other; Peter is so diabolical, our case had to be sealed. So my soon-to-be family heard all about my worst mistakes, and they were fed embellished stories and absolutely malicious lies—because Betsy did not allow me *to represent myself,* nor did she allow *Steven to represent himself.* She chose to communicate information *from Peter;* she also gave credence to an embittered and jealous ex-wife. Jo, in her obsession, used Betsy and the attention and energy that Betsy gave to Jo fueled Jo's legal firestorm, pre- and post-divorce. Jo kept her white-knuckled hold on Steven and on me. I endured this in order to preserve Steven's family dynamic.

After learning about the NCIS investigation and after Steven disclosed how suicidal he had become during the investigation, I lost my cool with Betsy. She continued to give heed to Jo's assertions, thereby hurting me and Steven. He tried to protect both of us, imploring to his judge to order Jo to stop disparaging us to the children and to his own family. The judge granted his motion and ordered all harassment and disparagement to stop; Jo would be in contempt of court if she continued to contact Betsy and engage in destructive talk. Steven had to go to court in an attempt to stop the toxic communication between his sister-in-law and his ex-wife.

As Steven continued to deteriorate in the aftermath of the investigation, I'd had enough of family politics. I confronted Betsy, the last portal through which information about Steven flowed freely to Jo and information from Jo flowed freely back to my soon-to-be family. In this conversation, Betsy relayed to me in a dismissive, minimizing and teaching sort of way, sort of way that "divorces are hard, and Jo and Steven will figure things out" that "the boys do talk," and that she knew that things "were not going well."

[The judge in Steven and Jo's supplementary custody and visitation orders stated, "Jo needs to understand that her behavior in placing the boys in the middle of the parties' disputes and more-or-less requiring them to report back to her on what Steven is doing can sometimes be more harmful psychologically to the children than the behavior she believes Steven is up to."]

Still Betsy insisted that she was "neutral" and "she wanted to stay in contact with [her] nephews." When I attempted to talk about Steven's side of the story I was met with, "I don't want to be involved. I don't want to hear anything." A few times, she even said, "I feel sorry for her." She went on to say that she could "accept [my] lifestyle as a lesbian. Living in a liberal state, [she] is good at accepting people for who they are." She did not ask one question; she didn't ask whether or not I was, indeed, a lesbian, nor did she ask about how Steven or I were doing. She simply defended her ongoing and public friendship with Jo.

Steven and I struggled through Betsy's blatant campaign against us, but we decided to forgive and forget and focus on moving forward. With Steven retiring soon, we looked for a new-found relationship with Betsy and her husband, Steven's brother, and planned to visit them with regularity.

At our wedding, a member of my family found it odd that when she spoke to Betsy and Ross about how much they loved, respected and were thankful for Steven, the couple remained silent and looked oddly uncomfortable.

Sometime later, I learned that Betsy and Jo were still communicating. I tried to shake it, but I became depressed and couldn't settle an uncomfortable feeling. I asked Betsy if she was *able to* cut off from Jo as even the slightest energy keeps the fire lit, and I wondered how vulnerable Steven and I could be with her if she insisted on communication with Jo. I received a voicemail the next day from Steven's brother scolding me as if I had misbehaved. Steven took a call from Betsy and she spent the entire conversation defending her communication with Jo, asking no questions, stating passionately that she "was only being neutral," and speaking as though she was a victim (I had interrupted a date night). She repeated herself, asking Steven to agree with her that I was the villain. I asked how vulnerable we could continue to be with her.

I realized that my depression stemmed from my betrayal of myself and from continuing to act like a victim. My fear of Betsy was paralyzing. Steven and I walked on eggshells, not speaking our thoughts and feelings for fear of the consequences within his family. Additionally, Steven had just dropped another six thousand dollars to litigate Jo's attempts to "Abate all Parental Contact." Steven, concerned about continued communication, ongoing timeshare litigation and months-long alienation from his boys, asked Betsy for an apology. In response, she mocked him for not having spoken to his boys in more than three months, claiming that she had done everything that she could to support Steven, requesting that he delete her contact information.

From a fearless perspective we should have simply let Betsy behave as she will and communicate with whom she likes, we shouldn't have asked anything of her. A healthier approach after observing hostile communication is to disengage, accepting shifts in the family dynamic until they are resolved. A few days later, Steven and I listened to a voice mail in which his brother says that he and Steven need to work together to make sure "Betsy doesn't receive any more communications [from me]."

Email 4/9/2013
"Hi Steven,
I've been communicating with Sabrina and hear you'll be moving soon.

How are things coming along? How do you feel about leaving AK? Will you be living at the base for awhile? As I recall your house will not be vacated until July.

Just thinking of you and wanted to let you know it. As I was chatting with Ross recently, he asked about you. I felt really sad not to be able to tell him all that is going on, but know that he and Betsy share info and I didn't want Betsy to share with Jo. If you happen to communicate with him, be sure not to say "don't tell Betsy" cause they have no secrets. I do think he'd like to hear from you if you have the opportunity to call.

Love you,
Mom"

Email 6/5/2013
"Hi Steven,

Thanks for the address. You must be frustrated with Jo or perhaps you're used to the same o, same o. Is she not in contempt of court? When the boys finally do arrive, I hope you have lots of fun all summer long…

Whatever is going on with Sabrina and Betsy I do hope it's being resolved. Betsy has now removed herself from my family group on social media so I do not have that access to my grandchildren. I'm sad about that. I think there's a lot of she said and she said, I hope all can be understood and everybody move on…Maybe by now Sabrina and Betsy have talked and things are better…

Take care.
I love you. Mom"

TWENTY-SIX

The Special Operator

Steven has been awarded three **BRONZE STARS:**

THE SECRETARY OF THE NAVY
Washington, D.C. 20350-1000

The President of the United States takes pleasure in presenting the BRONZE STAR MEDAL to

BOATSWAIN's MATE FIRST CLASS (SEA, AIR AND LAND)
STEVEN J. BROWN
UNITED STATES NAVY

For service as set forth in the following

CITATION:

For heroic achievement in connection with combat operations against the enemy as reconnaissance troop lead sniper and navigator while assigned as a member of a Joint Task Force conducting special operations in support of operation ENDURING FREEDOM from 29 April to 22 July 2003. Petty Officer Brown performed superbly during the successful execution of over 30 special operations missions that consisted of special reconnaissance, intelligence collection, and direct action compound assaults deep in the enemy territory, striking at the heart of senior Al Qaeda and Taliban leadership. His leadership and expertise in special reconnaissance, close quarter combat, mobility skills, and patrol tactics were vital to the successful capture of 10 enemy personnel greatly reducing the enemy's ability to operate in and extremely volatile region, Petty Officer Brown's contagious leadership and willingness to repeatedly go in harm's way were critical to the success of his unit's mission. His keen insight and effective use of innovative tactics in various situations established a new precedence for tactical leaders operating in Afghanistan. By his zealous initiative, courageous actions, and exceptional dedication to duty, Petty Office Brown reflected great credit upon himself and upheld the highest traditions of the United States Naval service.

Combat distinguishing device is authorized.

For the President
Signed by the Secretary of the Navy for the President

THE SECRETARY OF THE NAVY
Washington, D.C. 20350-1000

THE SECRETARY OF THE NAVY
Washington, D.C. 20350-1000

The President of the United States takes pleasure in presenting the BRONZE STAR MEDAL to

BOATSWAIN's MATE FIRST CLASS (SEA, AIR AND LAND)
STEVEN J. BROWN
UNITED STATES NAVY

For service as set forth in the following

CITATION:

For meritorious achievement in connection with combat operations against the enemy as a member of a Presidential Security Detail for a highly visible foreign head of state from 15 July to 15 Task Force conducting a protective service mission for a foreign head of state targeted by Taliban and Al Qaeda enemy forces. Petty Officer Brown's attention to detail and meticulous pre-planning ensured the safety of multiple personnel movements. His resolute action and tactical foresight during a four day, highly visible movement to a volatile and unstable region was paramount to the success of this high-risk operation. Additionally, he played a critical role while executing numerous counter surveillance missions in efforts to significantly enhance the safety of Presidential motorcades and the United States security force. His tactical expertise and leadership improved the overall security of the Protective Detail and his individual actions were directly responsible for saving the life of the foreign head of state while maintaining the stability of the fledgling transitional government. By his zealous initiative, courageous actions, and exceptional dedication to duty, Petty Officer Brown reflected great credit upon himself and upheld the highest traditions of the United States Naval Service.

For the President,
Secretary of the Navy

COMMANDER
NAVAL SPECIAL WARFARE COMMAND

The President of the United States takes pleasure in presenting the BRONZE STAR MEDAL (Gold Star in lieu of the Third Award) to

CHIEF BOATSWAIN's MATE FIRST CLASS (SEA, AIR AND LAND)
STEVEN J. BROWN
UNITED STATES NAVY

For service as set forth in the following

    CITATION:

        For heroic achievement in connection with combat operations against the enemy as an Assault Squadron Team Leader, Joint Task Force, in direct support of Operation ENDURING FREEDOM from 19 November 2004 to 20 November 2004. Chief Petty Officer Brown guided his four-man team in the execution of a complex and daring clandestine mission against a heavily armed and fortified Al-Qaeda command and control cell. His decisive actions during and following the contact resulted in a secure objective free of casualties, allowing for the safe extraction of the larger force. This operation provided a windfall of intelligence to the Joint Task Force for future combat operations. By his extraordinary guidance, zealous initiative, and total dedication to duty, Chief Petty Officer Brown reflected great credit upon himself and upheld the highest traditions of the United States Naval Service.

The Combat Distinguishing Device is authorized.

For the President,
Rear Admiral, United States Navy
Commander, Special Warfare Command

TWENTY-SEVEN

The Most Dangerous Operation of Steven's Career

Though Steven has earned some of the highest awards in the Navy, they do not reflect the most dangerous of his more than 250 operations. Though not awarded for this one, from Steven's perspective, and in his own words, this was the most dangerous:

"This operation (OP) took place mid-May 2006, [just prior, approximately four days, to the one where he earned the Silver Star].

The plan was to kill/capture a Taliban leader in the Kandahar area of Afghanistan.

Sniper team, assault team and blocking positions departed Bagram airfield, north of Kabul, on a C-130 to Kandahar. After landing in Kandahar we loaded into helicopters (HELO) CH-47's and flew to a forward operating base (FOB).

Received a last-minute intel dump on the target (TGT), loaded back up and flew to our insertion point.

Foot patrolled approximately 3 hours, in the desert, skirting small villages, dogs barking (used to that) crossed a dry riverbed and moved to a position where the assault team could get ready to hit the target. BR and I were leading the patrol on point. We pushed forward from the main body to observe a terrain feature that would provide a tactical advantage, overlooking the target compound that we preplanned to move to. While doing so we observed an individual stand up, sling an AK-47 overhead and walk down the terrain feature to the target compound, then a second person did the same.

I radioed what we observed to the Assault Troop Chief, ML. Once BR and I received word, the Assault Force was ready to move to the TGT, we moved out well ahead of the assault force, keeping an eye on the hilltop, staying quiet and looking for an alternative way to get the assault force to the TGT without being compromised. There was no other way to move around the 6' mud walls and noisy vegetation so we decided to stay on the original route.

The night was very dark, quiet, no wind, the ground was hard, about 25 yards separated BR and I from where we saw the two enemy fighters move from. BR and I were moving past the hill on our left, the target compound straight ahead of us, about 125 yards away. As the assault force closed the distance to the enemy position, I saw another fighter on the hilltop stand up and sling a PKM machine gun, then another with a PKM. I put the infrared laser from my rifle on the first guy. It was a very dark night, the laser easily seen through night vision goggles. I couldn't talk into my headset or the guys on top of the hill would hear me. I was using my laser to try to nonverbally communicate with the assault force. Two more fighters stood up and slung PKM's as the assault force approached. As soon as we saw a few more lasers from the main body on the fighters, BR and I engaged them.

The violence of action was intense, then BR and I began to take fire from in front of us. A rocket propelled grenade (RPG) hit the wall in front of us, then a couple more explosions, probably fragmentation grenades or booby traps being initiated from the RPG explosion. Small arms fire continued from our front, BR and I covered each other while moving back to the Assault Force. Once there, the entire force began to assault the hill and area outside the target compound. We got a call from our tactical operations center (TOC), watching and listening to all of this going on letting us know

He Married a Sociopath

there were 12-15 personnel moving in our direction from the other side of the TGT.

We are obviously postured for the fight, an air strike is called in, an A-10 strafes the enemy patrol. Don't know how many they took out, we continued receiving small arms fire. BR and I make it to the top of the hill with some of the assault force, the rest of the assault force covering down on the TGT and our six. We heard sporadic gun fire from our 10 to 2 o'clock. We are now searching the dead enemy fighters, on one of them we find a radio and another a set of binoculars, both items functional. There is talking on the radio, we give it to our interpreter (TERP) and he starts translating, saying they know Americans are in the area, get your guns, blah, blah, blah.

The call is made to assault the TGT. The TGT is explosively breached, entered, cleared, secured and searched. The clearance is pretty quick, the detailed search takes a while. The Taliban leader we were hunting was gone. We're still taking ineffective fire from somewhere and people keep talking on the enemy radio. Now the sun is starting to come up. A quick reaction force is overhead in a CH-47 from the FOB, it lands behind a tree line, the Rangers on board unass the bird, hop over a wall and make their way into a field. Communication is made with them and they begin to move towards the TGT with the wall separating their force from ours. They are contacted by the enemy and one of the Rangers is hit in the leg by small arms fire; they suppress the fire.

Our communicator initiates the call for a medical evacuation (MEDEVAC) while the Ranger is being treated. Still more talking on the enemy radio, I'm starting to become irritated that I can't figure out where the position this person is reporting from. The sun is now up. I move to a very exposed position that is near a small depression in the ground, where I have our TERP lay. I hear rounds cracking overhead—a noise one becomes very familiar with while going through sniper school pulling targets in the butts at the range. I know who ever is shooting can see me, they are just a bad shot. They keep talking; our TERP keeps translating. I'm using the binos from the dead guy to help observe. I look over at our TERP, his head is exposed, looking around, I say to him, not very politely to put his head down, you're no good to us if your dead. ML moves out to our position, let's me know a bird is inbound for the wounded ranger. Just then I see a head about 250 yards away, it disappears behind a 3' wall then I hear, blah, blah, blah on the radio the TERP is translating. It appears again, disappears, blah, blah, blah. Appears again, disappears, blah, blah, blah. Got you fucker. Switch from the binos to my riflescope. Still rounds cracking overhead. I hear the MEDEVAC in the distance, I think it will approach and land behind me where they dropped the quick reaction force (QRF), pick up the wounded guy and get out of here. I was wrong, I see it at my 2 o'clock moving over the TGT building, blah, blah , blah on the radio again. As the HELO is flying 200' almost directly over the position of the guy I've been watching, an enemy fighter stands up with an RPG, points it to the sky and then he drops to the ground. Another guy stands up looking down at the guy just dropped and he ends up down as well. The HELO lands, picks up the wounded ranger and takes off. ML and the comms guy are coordinating our HELO exfiltration. About five minutes go by, no small arms fire cracking overhead and no blah, blah, blah anymore. A few more minutes go by and blah, blah, blah starts again, only now it's a female voice. I ask the TERP what is she saying she sees and with what she saw her position had to be in a small village across the river about 600 yards away. I observed the area for a few minutes then we had to move to get picked up, never saw her. We are picked up and flown straight to Kandahar airfield, where we remained until night fall when a C-130 took us back to Bagram.

After we returned, cleaned up, ate, I began to reflect on last night. Would I have done anything different, on the OP, no. Before the OP, very much so. I found myself becoming complacent. This was my eighth deployment to Afghanistan or Iraq, while mission planning for this OP I had BR, new to my sniper team, create a route from where the HELO's dropped us off in the desert to the target, I did the same. After reviewing his route, it was easy to see it was better. Had we taken my route that night we would have been walking straight down a dry riverbed into an awaiting ambush on that hilltop. I probably wouldn't be writing this right now; even worse, I'm sure I would have gotten some of my brothers killed and wounded. Thank you, BR.

A few nights later this same crew left for the OP where I was awarded the Silver Star and three of my other Brothers were also awarded the Silver Star. BR was wounded by a frag grenade, awarded the Purple Heart and a Bronze Star with "V" for Valor. The rest of the crew was awarded Bronze Stars with "V". We got that Taliban leader that night; that was a hell of a night."

This operation is so important in relation to Steven's experience of what Jo has done to him. Answering the NCIS investigator's call created more anxiety and inner turmoil than his leadership of the operation. He had no control over the outcome—he couldn't determine what he was up against because it wasn't based in reality. The enemy was singularly focused on his destruction; he was alone in this battle—he didn't have his brothers.

TWENTY-EIGHT

Officer in Charge

Jo's intentional destruction of the American war hero is obvious. Her representation of Steven is removed from the reality of his career. As the NCIS investigation began, unbeknownst to him, Steven was being singled out for higher leadership within Naval Special Warfare (NSW).

Commander of the NSW Center, a Captain (O6) planning on commissioning a Naval Special Warfare Sniper School, asked Steven to put in a Warrant Officer package to become the first Officer in Charge of the NSW Sniper School. He had letters of support from higher ups within his chain of command, including other Warrant Officers. Steven submitted his package and was picked first from all of the Chiefs and Senior Chiefs. He had the strongest support from his chain of command, including from the Senior Warrant Officer in all of Naval Special Warfare.

This opportunity was perfect for us. It would bring him close to where I was employed. Steven could remain active duty and we could see each other on the weekends.

There were budget cuts and NSW could not move forward with the Sniper School plan in Indiana. Because of this, if he accepted, Steven would be placed on an East Coast Team and he would soon deploy.

At the same time that he was teetering close to a dishonorable discharge, he was asked to take a Warrant Officer position from some of the highest leadership in NSW.

TWENTY-NINE

Summer Visitation, 2013

Steven turned down the Warrant Officer opportunity, deciding to retire at twenty years of service as a Navy SEAL. He decompressed with a cross-country drive in his 1987 Volkswagen Westfalia, concluding his journey in Virginia Beach, where he was stationed for his last year before retirement. He stopped in Kentucky to pick up Junior and me and we travelled the rest of the way with him. While still in Kentucky, Steven and Junior waited in his van for the rain, which interrupted Junior's baseball game, to stop. Steven opened a safe, showing to Junior a ring, then asked him if it was okay to marry me, and for the three of us to move to Virginia Beach. Junior was very excited, but he kept the secret until Steven gave the ring to me.

We camped at New River Gorge, and there went white water rafting, climbing and hiking. Life is always an exciting adventure with Steven. On a very long hike, Steven suggested that we go off trail, down to the water. At this remarkable spot, near a class-five rapid, he got down on one knee and asked me to be his wife, and offered to me his very dear grandmother's ring. I had no way to expect this because we had already decided to get married. Steven's most romantic gesture as part of our engagement is that he tattooed latitude and longitude of this proposal spot onto his wedding finger as his wedding ring. He made sure that I knew that he meant forever. I was to him as his paternal grandmother was to his grandfather. To him, they are the epitome of soul mates and best friends.

Thomas and Jay came for their summer visitation in Virginia Beach at this time. We planned many activities for all three boys. We were excited to be a family, living under the same roof for the whole summer. Steven went back to court to limit Jo's contact with the boys to once per day. Jo was still calling and texting throughout the day and it was interfering with Steven's quality time with the boys; the judge agreed. Jo decided on a time of day, and she was limited to no more than thirty minutes each day. She called exactly on the minute of "her time" every day; it was only once so it was manageable. Considering how well things had gone during spring break, and how easily the three boys got along, we were optimistic.

We eloped on June 21, 2013 because the judge in my case required that we be married in order to move Junior. Having no one to watch the children and not wanting to leave them at the house, we dropped the boys off at the local water park (we had a season pass and went often). That evening when Steven's boys took their call from Jo, they must have relayed that Steven and I had married and they had been at the waterpark during our ceremony. The next day, Steven received a voicemail from Jo accusing us of abuse after leaving the boys unattended. She had already verified that we had been married, with the court house, and threatened to involve attorneys and social services; she followed through with both. Her attorney threatened action if Steven did this again, social services did not investigate.

Junior and I stayed for a few weeks and then returned to Kentucky to finish packing up our house. My brother helped me move from Kentucky to Virginia Beach; his wife and family met us at the house that Steven rented for the summer. When we all made it to the house, Steven and I asked my brother and sister-in-law out for dinner in order to thank them for their help. My sister-in-law stayed at the house with the boys; she said she wasn't hungry. Later that year, when I opened up to her about all that happened, she said that Thomas choked her son, four years old at the time, and that both of Steven's boys had bullied her son during spring break. She didn't say anything in the moment because she did not want to upset our new household.

I've never, before or since, experienced anything like I did with Steven's pre-teen and teenage boys. I was not (and am not) equipped, to deal with what happened during the next year. This was a more stressful beginning to our lives together than Steven and I could have imagined. Though Jo's contact with the boys was contained, her unleashed communications to Steven continued as they had.

Thomas (age 14) could not keep his hands off of Junior (age 9). Thomas incessantly put choke holds on his younger step-brother. Following a series of traumatic events perpetrated by Steven's boys, I reviewed our photos. Thomas almost always had his hands on Junior, usually with a choke hold around Junior's neck, while Junior stood on tiptoes trying to get his hands in between his neck and Thomas's arm. Steven's boys did not listen to me, not even to the smallest of requests, so I was unable to discipline them. Whenever I asked Thomas to turn off the video games, he ignored me. When I asked them to pick up their dirty socks, they stepped on the socks and smirked at me as they walked by. Both boys played video games for most of their waking hours, and I found them watching inappropriate movies with Junior. When I turned off these movies, reminding the older boys that Junior was not allowed to watch them, Jay replied with variations of, "I watched them when I was younger than Junior."

Steven's boys had been distant, and sometimes disrespectful with me during visitations. Their poor behavior toward me ramped up during this visit. Steven felt reluctant to discipline Thomas and Jay; he had spent so little time with them. In addition, he was afraid of consequences from Jo so both boys became uncontrollable.

Something else didn't seem right to me. Both boys had an insatiable need for Steven's affection. Even Thomas wanted Steven to hold him like a baby and rock him. Every time Steven sat down, one or the other of his boys climbed onto his lap, rubbing and kissing him. The boys talked constantly about how much they loved their father, using baby talk . Steven returned their affection, not noticing anything weird about it. They got plenty of affection from Jo, and commented that they slept with her. She posted on social media how happy it made her to wake up snuggled between her boys. In their divorce, the judge gave their king-sized bed to Jo after she argued, "My boys sleep with me, so I need the bigger bed." It's normal, during a divorce, for younger children to want to sleep in the same bed with their parents. I learned this during my family evaluations. In my divorce case, I was told NOT to allow this with Junior (and he was six years old at the time). I explained to Steven how odd his boys' behavior was, in both parents' homes, and expressed concern about the potential for false sexual allegations if he didn't create boundaries with them.

Steven and I were going through so much that a neighbor, who is also a friend recommended a therapist, whom I started seeing twice a week. Sometimes Steven and I went to therapy together, and sometimes he went on his own. He was very open to therapy and to working through everything with me; he even went to day-long retreats with me. Junior also went to therapy, periodically. It was time for Thomas and Jay to come with us. Our therapist knew the family backstory and had worked with me for many hours to help me deal with Steven's boys.

During one therapy session, when Thomas pushed and rubbed Junior, Junior pushed him off, clearly not wanting to be touched like this. I told Thomas to stop, but he did not. The therapist said to Steven, "Please tell Thomas to stop." Steven told him to stop, but minutes later, he began again. Both boys talked freely and often about "tea bagging." They made references to their penises and made noises as they rubbed their genitals on each other, simulating sexual acts. They wrestled, trying to rub their genitals on each other's faces. I brought all of this up in therapy because I was concerned for Junior; I thought that their behavior was highly sexualized and concerning and that we needed help handling the boys.

The following summer, Junior revealed that both boys talked a lot about sexual activities. Though they still all had a good time together (and Junior liked them), this was the beginning of Thomas and Jay's (age 11) systematic bullying of my son.

THIRTY

Cops at the Crack House

As much as you may want to save your child, you cannot rescue your child from the quicksand by jumping into the quicksand with them. If, in trying to rescue your child from quicksand you jump into the quicksand as well, you will simply both perish.
~Dr. Craig Childress

Steven's home in Virginia Beach was still occupied by renters, so Steven rented another house from one of his colleagues. We call it "the crack house" because there were sketchy individuals and cops outside, most nights. Jo notified attorneys that we had the children staying in a house across the street from a registered sex offender. We never let the boys go outside without us. We didn't have furniture because I had sold mine and the military was holding onto Steven's until we could move into our house.

We returned to "the crack house" after a day at the local water park and dinner out. Steven's dad and stepmother were visiting and stayed at a nearby hotel. They visited with us for a while, at the house, and left at around 10:00 p.m. After I put my son to bed,

Steven's boys stayed up to watch a movie with us. When Jo called, the boys went up to their room to talk with her.

She required that they take her calls away from anyone else; she interrogated them and didn't want us to overhear. The judge in Steven and Jo's custody case identified this tendency in her and ordered her to stop the behavior—stating that it was unhealthy for the boys. The judge had even included the following statement in the *Findings of Fact and Conclusions of Law* in 2011, "Neither parent shall question the children about the other parent. The parents cannot put the children in the middle and have them as reporting parties." In 2012 the judge stated, "While it is not clear to this court whether the boys simply offer up information about their dad when back home later with their mother (or when she speaks to them on the phone during their visits to Kodiak) or rather, if she quizzes them on everything he is doing, putting the children in the middle of their parent's arguments is specifically forbidden in the custody order." Steven thinks that Jo used real military-style interrogation techniques; asking the same question repeatedly and for months. Scientific studies show that the parental brainwashing of children in severe PAS cases is much like techniques used by cult leaders. To counteract the brainwashing requires methods similar to what is used in cult indoctrination deprogramming [9, 32].

Steven listened at the door and, when he determined that yet another interrogation was happening, he told the boys to come downstairs, that there was no reason for them to take the call upstairs. Suddenly, Jay ran into the downstairs bathroom and locked the door. I knew exactly what was happening—Jo was setting us up. I banged on the door and when Jay refused to open it, I told Steven to take it off the hinges. By then, Jay was screaming "Help me, help me!" Steven got the door open, took the phone from him and hung up. Steven had the boys sit down and I said, "The police will be here soon and all of you could be taken from us, including my son." Everyone was quiet and I said, "She is definitely calling the police and I need to let them know the backstory." So I called. The following is the transcript from this call.

He Married a Sociopath

```
Printed for: ADM2/1531                                    Fri Sep 20 16:31:23 2013

CHIQ    PAGE NO.0001 1531   ADM2    09-20-2013 16:27
                    VA BEACH LAW CALLS FOR SERVICE TRAN
                    CALLS-FOR-SERVICE INQUIRY RESPONSE
-----------------------------------------------------------------------

INITIATE:   23:03:29 07-19-2013    CALL NUMBER:      132001347
ENTRY:      23:05:21               CURRENT STATUS:   CLOSED
DISPATCH:   23:09:27               PRIMARY UNIT:     428B
ON SCENE:   23:13:28               JURISDICTION      P
CLOSE:      23:47:13               DISPOSITION:      N

LOCATION:   835 CRASHAW ST  , ( COLERIDGE CT & CAMPION AV )
DAREA:      4TH
BEAT:       428                    TYPE:     DOMS
RD:         458016                 PRIORITY: 2
FIRE:       HF379J

CP:         MS BROWN
ADDRESS:
PHONE:      ████████████████

07-19-2013
23:05:21 ST2  ENTRY    TEXT:COMPL STATES HER KIDS ARE HERE IN VB WITH HER EXHUSB
                       AND AND HIS GF..COMPL STATES HER ●YO SON CALLED HER AND
                       LEFT THE LINE OPEN SO COMPL COULD HERE GF YELLING AT HER
                       11YO SON..THE ●YO LOCKED HIMSELF IN THE BATHROOM.. \NAME
                       :MS BROWN \PH: ████████ . (MTF)
23:05:54 P4   HOLD
23:06:54 ST2  SUPP     TEXT:COMPL STATES THAT SHE COULD HEAR YOUNGEST STAING HE J
                       UST WANTED SOME MEDICINE FOR HIS EARS..COMPL STATED THAT
                       HER SON WAS STATING HE IS SCARED OF THEM..THE COMPL WOULD
                       LIKE FOR OFCRS TO GO..COMPL STATED SHE COULD (MTF)
23:07:26 ST2  UPDATE   TYPE:ASTC-->DOMS DTYPE:AST CITIZEN-->DOMESTIC
23:07:26 ST2  SUPP     TEXT:HERE BOTH KIDS GETTING YELLED AT BY THE ADULTS AND T
                       HEN THE LINE DISCONNECTED
23:07:57 ST2  UPDATE   PRI:3-->2
23:07:57 ST2  SUPP     TEXT:COMPL STATES THIS IS AN ONGOING ISSUE..THIS OCCURED
                       WITHIN 10 MIN..
23:08:35 P4   HOLD
23:09:27 P4   DISPATCH 427C 427B
23:09:27 P4   ID       427C (████)BUCK,JUSTIN S
23:09:27 P4   ID       427B (████)SHELTON,JONATHAN P.
23:09:29 ST2  SUPP     TEXT:COMPLS EXHUSBAND IS STEVEN BROWN..W/ DARK HAIR BLUE
                       EYES 6'0 TALL...COMPL STTAES THE SUBJ IS A NAVY SEAL AND
                       HAS ALOT OF WEAPONS..THE FEMALE IS SABRINA WALSH..W/F RED
                       HAIR MAYBE 5'4..COMPL STATES THAT THEY ARE ALWAYS DRINKI
                       NG..
23:09:56 P4   ENROUTE  427C
23:09:56 P4   ENROUTE  427B
23:10:21 P4   BACK-ER  427B 428B
23:10:21 P4   ID       428B (████)HAMANN,PAUL E
23:11:18 ST2  SUPP     TEXT:COMPL STATES THAT SHE HAS FULL CUSTODY OF THE KIDS..
                       THE MALE HAS VISITATION..THE COMPL IS IN FLORIDA..COMPL S
                       TATED THAT THE KIDS ARE TOLD NOT TO CALLL THE COMPL AND T
                       HREATENS TO HIT THE CHILDREN IF THEY CALL THE COMPL..
23:11:51 ST2  SUPP     TEXT:CPS HAS BEEEN INVESTIGATING THE MALE SUBJ IN FLORIDA
                       ..

CHIQ    PAGE NO.0002 1531   ADM2    09-20-2013 16:27
                    VA BEACH LAW CALLS FOR SERVICE TRAN
                    CALLS-FOR-SERVICE INQUIRY RESPONSE

23:13:18 ST2  SUPP     TEXT:COMPL WOULD LIKE IF OFCRS WOULD CONTACT HER BY PHONE
                       TO LET HER KNOW OF HER CHILDRENS WELFARE..CAN BE REACHED
                       AT ████████
23:13:28 P4   ONSCENE  427B
23:14:20 V492 ONSCENE  428B
                              Page 1
```

```
Printed for: ADM2/1531                                    Fri Sep 20 16:31:23 2013
23:14:25 V602 ONSCENE    427C
23:15:00 ST2  MISC       .1347, COMPL JUST STATED THAT HER EXHUSBAND HIDES THE ALC
                         OHOL..THE COMPL STATED SHE COULD HER THE FEMALE YELLING A
                         T THE KIDS COME OUT OF THERE YOUR GOING TO GET US INTO TR
                         OUBLE WITH CPS AGAIN
23:16:43 S3   MISC       .1347, SABRINA BROWN /#859.28?.7271 CALLING FROM INSIDE W
                         ORRIED THAT THE CHILDS BIOLOGICAL MOTHER WOULD CALL THE C
                         OPS ON THEM. SHE ADVSD THE CHILDS MOTHER WAS ON THE PHONE
                         WITH COMPS STEPSON, AND THE MOTHER TOLD THE SON TO LOCK
                         HIMSELF IN THE BATHROOM AND CONVINCED HIM TO BE SCARED. S
                         ABRINA SAID SHE WANTED AN OFFICER TO COME TO THE HOUSE TO
                         INTERVIEW THE CHILDREN AND CHECK THE CONDITIONS SO PD CA
                         N SEE FOR THEMSELVES EVERYTHING IS OK. I ADVSD SABRINA PO
                         LICE WERE ALREADY ONSCENE OF HER HOUSE.
23:41:13 V602 ONSCENOK   427B
23:41:13 V602 ONSCENOK   428B
23:41:13 V602 ONSCENOK   427C
23:44:30 V602 INSRVICE   427C
23:45:33 V425 INSRVICE   427B
23:47:10 P4   MISC       428B, PLS CLR, NR. NO INDICATIONS THAT ANY BODY WAS UNDER
                         THE INFLUENCE OF ALCOHOL. SPOKE WITH BOTH OF THE BOYS,
                         , SEPERATELY FROMT THE ADULTS, BOTH DENIED B
                         EING MISTREATED OR NOT PROVIDED WITH PROPER TREATMENT. SP
                         OKE WITH THE COMPL VIA      PHONE, SHE REITERATED WHAT S
                         HE HAD TOLD CALL TAKER. I ASSURED HER EVERYTHING WAS WELL
                         AT CS LOCATION. TKS[07/19/13234710001]
23:47:13 P4   CLEAR      428B N
23:47:13 P4   CLOSE      428B N

OPERATOR ASSIGNMENTS:         ST2          STALCH,AMBER M.
                              P4           WESTBY,PATRICIA A
                              V492         HAMANN,PAUL E
                              V602         BUCK,JUSTIN S
                              S3           SANSONE,JONATHAN
                              V425         SHELTON,JONATHAN P.
AS OF 07-19-2013-23:47:10     P4           ASPER,TIA

**** REPORT COMPLETED ****
```

Jay's ear was bothering him and Steven prepared to do a peroxide treatment on him, something that the SEALS do often and he already had everything needed out and ready. The police officers, after interviewing the children, told us that it was good that I had called and even offered to help if there were future false allegations. Having been told by Jo that Steven was a dangerous Navy SEAL, the police surrounded the house with lights out, and approached the scene assuming a high threat level, as though he was armed, dangerous and intoxicated. It could have been even more traumatic for all of us than it already was.

I called Steven's stepmother to tell her what happened.

She said, "But everything was fine and everyone happy when we left."

I said, "That's typical of Jo, especially because everything was fine."

She said, "I can hear how upset you are in your voice; your voice is shaking."

I said, "This is our life, it will not stop with her."

I was glad that they had seen how detached Jo was from reality and how her interference was damaging all of us. Maybe things would be okay again with them now that they saw first-hand what we were up against.

When social services or police are called to a scene or become involved in family matters there is no sure outcome; anything can happen. Because of Jo, I had been so dangerously close to losing my son. That night, Steven and I had our first conversation about whether or not it was in anyone's best interest to have more visitation with his boys. Jo's interferences were that bad—for everyone.

THIRTY-ONE

I'm Devastated

Steven and I had so much baggage, from our first regrettable marriages, that neither of us thought we would get married again, but things kept progressing.

When we moved in together and then eloped, to be completely transparent with one another, something that neither of us had done in our previous marriages. We decided that we would have open access to one another's phones and computers and shared passwords.

In the fall of 2013, I found Steven's old phone. In it, I found hundreds of text messages, from Christmas 2011, between Steven and a woman who lived in Alaska. This discovery devastated me for several reasons. She was, at the time, in the public eye and a professional woman, he was saying some of the exact same things to her that he had to me and it was obvious that she was the one to stop messaging. Was I his second choice?

By the time Steven got home from work I was beside myself with heartache. He assured me that she was "Plan B" if we didn't work out, which did nothing to soothe my anguish. He told me that the relationship involved a couple of kisses and was not sexual. I replied that an emotional connection is far worse than just a physical relationship. I got a bottle of vodka, locked myself in the bathroom and sat in the bathtub the entire weekend. What in the world was I going to do now? I had just moved my son in with this man and we were already married. This, in combination with the drama surrounding Jo and his boys was pushing me back onto the ledge. By the end of the weekend, I decided that I would have walked away, if not for Junior. He loved Steven, and I couldn't hurt my son. Steven has always been an excellent father to Junior. I stayed, but I was not done nursing this new wound.

I found the woman's husband, an attorney, online. I called him and left a message. He called me right back and we talked for hours. He had found the text messages, as well, when he and the woman were engaged. He explained that Steven was one of three men with whom she had cheated. He believed that she and Steven were not physical, though she had been with the other two men. She had told him the same story that Steven had told me: they had met twice in person and the second visit he stayed at her place. She went upstairs after a movie and Steven slept on the couch. It was obvious to Steven that he was supposed to follow her; she had not left a blanket or pillow for him. Still, he chose to stay on the couch and left in the morning. Though he was on his way to see me, the text messages continued.

Her husband told me that he couldn't take it anymore. She was an alcoholic and, in his words "She's either at my throat or at my feet." He pointed me to several stories about her very public and publicized drunkenness. His portrayal of her reminded me of Jo; if Steven had continued his relationship with her, he would have found himself in a familiar situation again—the husband agreed. He said that Steven had dodged a bullet.

The husband went on to tell me that he had just filed for divorce and things had gotten ugly. He asked if Steven would provide an affidavit, if necessary, speaking to her character; he had asked the other men as well. She had thrown her missed opportunities with Steven and the others in her husband's face. Steven agreed to write an affidavit—probably to appease me—but the woman backed down and her husband did not need it after all. Years later, when the website that Steven and I started went live, "Steven Brown" and "Navy SEAL" appeared together online for the first time. When the woman saw this, she emailed Steven. Though it was obvious on our website that he is married, she stated that she missed him and left personal contact information asking for him to get in touch with her. Steven did not respond, deleted the message and told me about the email. I *did* reply to her to make certain that she understood our boundaries.

THIRTY-TWO

Repair Work and Remembering

I was overwhelmed by Jo and actually felt her presence in the Virginia Beach house, as if it was cursed. When Steven's mother came to visit, she kept Jo at the forefront of our conversations. Steven hadn't wanted her to visit, but I insisted; he had been instrumental in repairing my relationships with my family and I wanted to be the same sort of support for him. His mother slept until noon, she woke only to stand at the kitchen counter, in her pajamas, flipping through pictures of Steven and Jo and the boys, trying to understand what went wrong. She talked negatively about Jo—she had seen how badly Jo treated Steven from the beginning. She had confronted Steven about how quickly he had married Jo, questioning whether or not he really knew her.

Between the neighbors and Steven's mother, I was hearing or thinking about Jo most of the time. It was not healthy and my well-being deteriorated further. Steven's mother went to therapy with us, but didn't take responsibility for her part in their unhealthy relationship. She insisted Steven start treating her better (pulling her chair out from the dinner table and pushing it back for her). Steven told her it was time to leave.

For my entire life, I had been trapped in small places with limited resources. My instinct was to run away when I was hurt and felt unwanted. This time, I dug in, and not just for Junior, I was able to recognize all of the good in my relationship with Steven.

Shortly after we met, Steven invited me to one of his closest friend's wedding in Santa Barbara—they had met at BUD/s and been friends ever since. Steven was bringing me into his life; this was one of his friends he had not invited to his wedding to Jo. He had purchased a Volkswagen van and this friend picked it up for him and stored it at his house. Steven flew me to Santa Barbara to meet him. We camped in his new vehicle, met up with the soon-to-be married couple, attended the wedding and then drove up *California Highway One* to Washington state, from which he got on the ferry and continued to Alaska while I flew home to Kentucky. He cooked spaghetti in a bag, made a fire in pouring rain over which he cooked bratwursts for us; we visited with other of his lifelong friends and I tried sushi for the first time. It was the most exciting vacation I had ever experienced, and Steven perfectly planned every detail. On this trip, Steven said that he knew that we would get married. He had not said this to the other woman; I was his first choice. Steven is the most interesting person I have ever met and has had more life experiences than anyone else I know, and we were planning a shared life of travel and new adventures. It was right to stay for Junior and for ME—Steven and I are life partners.

THIRTY-THREE

At Last

At our wedding, our first dance was to *At Last* by Etta James. At last we found each other; at last we were married to the loves of our lives. It was a long road and, often, I didn't think that we would or should continue, but after all of it, we found ourselves dancing, with our hearts completely full. Steven wore his Dress Blues with his awards on his breast; I was so proud and felt more beautiful than I had ever felt before. It was the perfect day. Our venue was the oldest plantation in South Carolina, our families were there, everyone was happy (or so they seemed), and the weather unnaturally balmy.

I tried to make it perfect, setting up appointments for family to get their hair and make-up professionally done, including family as wedding participants. I would have chosen a date early in December, but Jo would not relent on visitation so it had to be during court-ordered visitation. Steven's boys were scheduled to arrive on December twenty-first, the winter solstice—we eloped on the summer solstice so this would have been beautiful symmetry. However, we were hesitant to count on their on-time arrival, so we decided on Sunday the twenty-second to ensure that they would be there. As expected, they arrived late, and not on the original flight that Steven had booked. Being so close to Christmas, many of our close friends were unable to join us. We accepted that the wedding would be more of a family affair. I am forever grateful to the friends and family that did attend our wedding—despite Jo and Peter's attempts to ruin our day, the event was beautiful and unforgettable.

Peter had visitation with Junior following our wedding day for the three days, so my brother met Peter and delivered Junior to him. Peter traveled with our two older daughters for this visitation. He tried to communicate with me extensively about plans, drop offs and concerns—on my rehearsal day, wedding day and right afterwards.

> Email 12/22/2013 at 10:28PM:
> *"Sabrina,*
> *I have tried several times to reach Junior by phone this evening. Is he available for a brief phone call? I want to talk to him about the exchange tomorrow morning at 10am.*
> *I haven't received a reply from you regarding the exchange. Where would you like to do the public exchange tomorrow morning? His sisters and I are certainly looking forward to spending this minimal time with Junior at Christmas in South Carolina.*
> *Please reply as soon as you receive this message this evening, at this late hour, to finally promote a modicum of transparency for Junior's sake.*
> *Peter"*

> Email 12/23/2013 at 3:27PM (from me):
> *We are keeping it simple and will go with the judge's orders and meet where your letter said.*

> Email 12/29/2013 at 9:32PM:
> *"Sabrina,*
> *…I will try calling simply to touch base with Junior in some way. Please keep in mind, for Junior's sake not mine, the cruciality of the father-son relationship. Attempts to substitute a father generally are not only unproductive, but rather serve as a detrimental force in the development of a boy.*

I hope in 2014, as an academician, you will pay heed to recent literature (see for example; Kay Hymowitz, "Boy Trouble" in City Journal) and dramatically increase my access to Junior, again for Junior's sake.

Your email from Myrtle Beach about an exchange: more "flexibility" with your daughters for more access to Junior, like some exchange of commodities was out of bounds on several fronts.

You stated the Judge is regularly asking about your relationship to your daughters in court proceedings. I don't have any recollection of these exchanges. My understanding is clearly that I was the last one to try to re-introduce the girls into the court proceeding in October 2012, when I wanted to have my sole responsibility for our daughters factored into the child support calculation. Recall, the Judge dismissed this entirely and closed the door on any consideration of the girls, having both crossed the 18-threshold.

The other aspect of the email I found baffling involves your efforts in August 2013, when, through the attorney you pay, you attempted to salvage something from your false allegation against me in court. You presented a document asking that we both stick to considerations of Junior in our correspondence, yet it was you that introduced a conversation concerning our daughters on December 24th.

I would like to Skype tomorrow at 8pm to make up for this evening. Please let me know.

Thank-you,
Peter"

On our wedding day, Jo sent a barrage of calls, text messages and emails—they came overwhelmingly. Neither of our ex-spouses could leave us alone during the best day of our lives.

My parents gave to us a three-day honeymoon, of sorts. We couldn't have a real one because of Steven's visitation. The first night, Jo would not stop contacting Steven. He turned off his phone. When he turned it back on the next day it was full of Jo's threatening communications. I threw his phone off of the balcony and into the pool. I could not take it anymore. The silence was wonderful.

THIRTY-FOUR

New Year's Eve: Jo's Vengeance Manifests in Thomas

Children tended to make stronger alliances with the more emotionally dysfunctional parent, who was more likely to be the mother…children in strong alignments forfeited their childhood by merging psychologically with a parent who was raging, paranoid, or sullenly depressed [paraphrased].
~Dr. J.R. Johnston, *Impasse of Divorce*

Steven divorced in May 2011 and I divorced in August 2011; and now, we were ringing in 2014. Neither Peter nor Jo had lessened their attacks toward us; their focus remained directly on the two of us.

On New Year's Eve, Junior was really hurt. Thomas, pointed a loaded BB-type gun at Junior's head. Later, Thomas, trained in jujitsu, choked Junior to unconsciousness. Junior "tapped out" nine times and we think Thomas only let go when he felt Junior go limp. Junior thought he was going to die; Thomas had done this many times before, but would let go when Junior "tapped out"—this time was different. This happened while we were eating dinner with neighborhood friends at 8:15p.m.; guests had arrived at 7:30 pm, and, guests were gone by 9:00p.m. because Junior was not feeling well at all and he was upset.

At 3:00a.m., after arguing for hours about what to do, Steven and I decided that we needed to alert the authorities and document this event. Thomas was clearly escalating, an indication that his violence was going to continue to escalate. In many states, including Virginia, strangulation is an automatic Felony; in Virginia the charges come from the Commonwealth. We did not know this at the time that we called; we were asking for advice. Upon learning this information, Steven thought he was saving Thomas's life, if this had happened after eighteen, the scenario would have been much worse. We wanted there to be an intervention in the home with Jo. We observed many risk factors for violence perpetration and victimization, one being Jo's constant disparagement of their father, telling them that he had replaced them with Junior. Additionally, his two boys were isolated and spent most of their free time playing the most violent video games on the market.

The police interviewed all five of us. This is from the official police report after interviewing Junior:

> IN THE CITY OF VIRGINIA BEACH, THOMAS BROWN, AGE 14, DID ON ABOUT 12/31/2013 UNLAWFULLY AND FELONIOUSLY, WITHOUT CONSENT, IMPEDE THE BLOOD CIRCULATION OR RESPIRATION OF [JUNIOR WALTON], AGE 10, BY APPLYING PRESSURE TO THE NECK OF SAID PERSON RESULTING IN WOUNDING OR BODILY INJURY, IN VIOLATION OF 18.2-51.6 OF THE 1950 CODE OF VIRGINIA AS AMENDED. THOMAS WAS CHARGED WITH DOMESTIC ASSAULT BY STRANGULATION.

Thomas was arrested and taken to the juvenile detention center to appear in court the following day. Thomas called Jo when he got there. I did not call Peter. I was worried that he would take Junior from me because this could prove that Junior wasn't safe with us. The summer before, Thomas had beaten Junior with closed fists; it had taken Junior some time to catch his breath and Junior sustained injuries as a result. I was afraid for Junior's safety and thought Thomas to be violent and dangerous by this point. Later I was told, over and over, by Steven's family members that this was just another case of "boys being boys." I refused to accept this; I was going to protect my son.

Jo contacted Steven, continuously blaming Junior, saying that he had hit Thomas with a *Nerf* bat and that Thomas was simply protecting himself from Junior—who had just turned ten. She accused Steven of ruining Thomas's life and that he should know better. We believe that when she did not get what she perceived to be an adequate response, from Steven, she contacted Peter.

> Email 1/1/2014 at 5:35PM:
> "*Sabrina Brown:*
> *I spoke a few minutes ago to a Sergeant from the Virginia Beach Police Department. I was given an outline of a report you filed with Virginia Beach Police sometime after midnight, this morning. The report apparently involves Thomas Brown, Steve Brown's son visiting from Florida, and involves our son.*
> *I have been instructed to contact the overnight Sergeant after 10pm this evening to gain more information (the overnight Sergeant is apparently able to speak to the report filed by Officer B, who works overnight).*
> *I am baffled by a complete lack of contact regarding Junior's status. It has been approximately 18-hours since you contacted the Virginia Beach Police. What is Junior's current condition? Was he taken to the ER (Please scan/email me a copy of the medical report)? What is the next step in this proceeding?*
> *Thank-you for your prompt attention to this matter. I am concerned for Junior's well-being.*
> *Peter Walton"*

I was in a complete panic about what would happen with Peter. I thought he would take the stance that Steven and I weren't protecting Junior and take me back to court for full custody, so I downplayed the incident with Peter.

Email 1/1/2014 at 7:13PM (from me):
It sounds like you have all the information through Steve's ex-wife and in talking to the police. You are scheduled to Skype with Junior at 8:30 tonight. I expected that he would tell you what happened though he is doing great today. No medical treatment to report.

Email 1/2/2014 at 9:53 AM
"Steve you have to help Thomas today. You have to remember who is really important. If you paint him the way Sabrina and you did in that letter, he will go to trial. You now how serious this is. Thomas is a good kid, period. Junior was swinging at bat at other kids. Help him!! This will effect Thomas's whole life. Make it right. Do the right thing, please.

Thank you, Jo Brown"

The judge ruled that Thomas take the first available flight back to Florida and that he and Junior be kept apart. Thomas, on the way back to our home, told Steven that it was fun in jail, the food was good, and he just played video games the whole time. When he came into the house, he immediately went up to Junior, grabbed him and looked as though he was going to put him in a choke hold again; Steven pulled him away before anything happened and I removed Junior from the house.

Email 1/2/2014 at 4:34 PM (from me, to Peter):
FYI: Thomas is on his way back to Florida. There will be a trial at an unknown time. Do you have a copy of the report yet?

I'm a little confused. I'm wondering why you would be in communication with Steve's ex-wife who does not see anything wrong with Junior being choked. She sent an email this morning saying Junior deserved what he received from Thomas. She regularly mocks your son. Thomas is going back into a chaotic environment instead of getting the help he needs here, under supervision, in part because of Jo's distorted communication with you. Because you familiarized me with what it feels like to be strangled, I took this very seriously and took action to protect Junior and have cared for him following. His stepfather saw that there needed to be a serious intervention, as well, even sending his own son to detention for Junior's protection, without hesitation. In other words, you are helping a woman that has done nothing but try and stop Thomas from facing consequences.

I am asking you to get on the side of Steve and myself and as Junior's father do something to help instead of hurt. Confront her about the blatant disregard for your son. Why aren't you angry at her for trying to block Steve and I simply protecting Junior? There are programs here that he would have immediately been forced to begin. This liaison is not helping Junior.

One week later we had to take Junior to the emergency room because his voice had not returned to normal and he continued to have pain in his throat.

Email 1/7/2014 (to Peter, Jo and Parent Coordinators, from me):
Peter,

Junior's symptoms continued to persevere so I made an appointment with his pediatrician here. He advised that we take Junior to the children's hospital in Norfolk immediately. Steve and I rushed him to the ER this morning and we are just home now. I would've communicated earlier but there was not cell service in the hospital. They have your information and are expecting a call from you. I will provide all details from our iCloud account. The attending physician there said that this was an assault and they would've involved police if we hadn't already and will be contacting Florida in an attempt to get Thomas the help he needs. Jo is opposed to treatment. He would've begun immediately if he stayed here....Feel free to contact Junior this evening....We appreciate you using our iCloud account after the first request and as an example of Jo's hostility, threats and argumentative posture, at the smallest of requests, she continues to respond at level 100. Jo has not lessened her attacks toward us one degree. It is baffling that she can't be professional at this point. I suspect she has never worked as a professional and doesn't know how. Of course this is hurting her sons and Thomas a symptom of her obvious rage, but now this is affecting your son. She is creating a circus besmirching and making light of this situation to anyone that will listen. We can only imagine what is to come considering Steve has been dealing with his, at this level, since 2004, when he tried to leave her the first time for this behavior/personality disorder.

I also appreciate how cordial you and Steve have become; this helps Junior. Jo's outright hostility toward me and now Junior is out of control. She is making it worse.

Thank you for your help in this matter, Sabrina

I assume Peter and Jo communicated after I sent that email because Peter's cordial conduct subsided after this email and he sided with Jo even more tenaciously.

When Thomas appeared before the judge and Jo telephonically, she disparaged me using information from my sealed divorce case.

Email 1/11/2014

"Jo,

You can probably imagine how worried I've been not even hearing that my sons arrived in Florida or speaking to them in any way since I put them on their planes. They are probably not only missing me, but their brother as well. Jay and Junior had a tearful parting. It looks as though you have blocked me from even their Facebook accounts. I look forward to FaceTime at my regular scheduled time.

I also want to bring something else to your attention and that of your attorney. Sabrina's divorce case is a sealed case. Sabrina's judge has acted quite sharply on several occasions about any information being released because of the nature of her ex-husband's motions. He and his attorney were reprimanded about what was being written and Sabrina has already disproved his false allegations; she should not have to ever again. You have quoted from these motions, not orders, in many emails and now under oath in court. Additionally, her ex has strict orders about his communication about and to her and seems to be going around those orders and using you to do so. We plan to bring these issues before her judge as soon as we are back in Lexington.

I was quite shocked to learn of your continued disparagement of me and my wife, even after orders, by not only you, but also your parents. The most concerning is to my 93-year-old grandfather and 89-year-old grandma. It seems it is nothing other than malicious to tell them that our wedding was a sham and we were married in June. To tell them I have to be escorted onto base doesn't even make sense; an obvious outright lie. To tell them I am being forced out of the military, also an outright lie and very malicious. I turned down warrant officer to retire and I am thrilled to finally be able to take this action. And after all that, to ask for money from them for a private attorney is really just hard to believe. Thomas's public defender was more than adequate.

Steven"

Jo's mother and stepfather called Steven's 93-year-old grandfather and 89-year-old grandmother to tell them stories of Steven's "dishonorable discharge" from the military and having to "be escorted onto base," and they were devastated. Of course, Steven's grandparents believed the stories; it's unfathomable that adults would be so malicious. Jo's mother and stepfather told them that our beautiful December wedding, the one that they had attended and thoroughly enjoyed, was a sham and that we had been hitched for months—we hadn't wanted anyone to know. They also asked them for money, to pay for attorneys, because of what Steven and I had done, saying Steven's grandparents (with whom they were talking with) needed to protect their great-grandson from us and that Jo was out of money.

It's not unusual for me to receive work-related calls so the second time a specific number appeared, I answered. There was someone on the other line and the line stayed open for several minutes, but nothing was said. As I continued to listen, an answering machine started to play...It was Jo's stepfather; I listened to the message—they stated their names and directions to leave a message—and then I hung up.

Steven called his grandparents and explained that he had been the first picked Warrant Officer in 2013 but decided to turn it down as we were not interested in his return to an East Coast Team to deploy. They were relieved and filled with righteous anger. Steven's grandmother, with whom I connected deeply and immediately, had seen Jo for who she was in 2004, when Steven first left. Her distrust of and distain for Jo had not changed. She told me that when Steven returned home from a deployment, Jo met him at the door with the children, immediately asking him to take them and delivering a list of "to dos." There was no transition; Steven's grandmother saw that it was only about Jo. Jo did not consider Steven's valiant actions, his need for recovery, or how she could help him transition back into normal life.

THIRTY-FIVE

Thomas

Because there was a documented injury following the strangulation, Thomas's case could not be dropped. Thomas was ordered to come back for a hearing.

Email: 2/22/2014 (from me):

Attorney R,

Thank you for all of your assistance with getting Thomas the help he needs!

Sorry for the delay in getting Junior's medical records to you. The last two pages from the x-ray and scope do indicate mild subglottic stenosis and narrowing of the subglottic airway. This was a week after the event.

We were wondering if we could get a copy of the orders for Thomas to receive treatment? We would like to send them to our civil attorney in Florida, where Thomas resides, to ensure the focus stays on the treatment program and that his mom does not continue to interfere with timeshare and resisting the process for healing.

Many thanks in advance for all of your help!

Sincerely, Sabrina Brown

Email: 2/22/2014

> *"Thank you for this information.*
>
> *I spoke with Thomas's attorney briefly on Friday and he wanted to speak with his client about the possibility of treatment; he wasn't able to state whether or not his client was insisting on a trial or if he'd be interested in complying with Court ordered treatment. I'm awaiting a response from him. If I don't receive anything by email then I assume he will discuss such information on Monday morning.*
>
> *I will definitely keep you updated if there's any new developments.*
>
> *Sincerely,*
>
> *Attorney R."*

When we went to the courthouse for Thomas's hearing, Jo, her stepfather, her mother and Jay were also there with Thomas. Both Jay and Thomas had hoodies on and had the hoods pulled over their heads. They looked down so that Steven and I could not see their faces. Jo had security following us, saying that we were dangerous, and she and her family needed protection from us. The most alarming part of this picture was that when Jo sat down in the courthouse, waiting for Thomas to be heard, her boys sat on either side of her, hugging her and comforting her. The way that they held her was reminiscent of a "significant other." She was demonstrably very emotional the entire day and clearly leaning on her children. Though they had driven all the way from Florida, the boys were not permitted to even look in the direction of their father.

Thomas was court ordered to complete an anger management program. We could have moved forward with felony charges, but our focus was on treatment for Thomas; for him to better handle frustrations, anger and his general emotional state. He was ordered to have only non-hostile interactions with Junior.

THIRTY-SIX

Peter and Jo

The week that we moved into our house in Virginia, Junior found a best friend whose parents happen to be fantastic people. We enjoyed spending time with them and felt that they would be life-long friends. The boys were two little blonde-haired man-cubs, the way they played outdoors and climbed everything. One night they were running and jumping at the friend's house and the other boy accidentally kicked Junior's eye. Both parents came to our house immediately concerned and apologetic. Junior was uncomfortable for a couple of days, but his eye healed completely.

Email 2/1/2014

"Ms. Brown:

Junior appeared on our Skype session on Thursday evening (January 30th) with a significant mark across his right eye and swelling on the same eyelid. Further the eyelid was quite red. I was taken aback and I inquired, of course —perhaps you were listening. Junior reported his friend …. while jumping on his bed clocked him in the eye with an errant foot. I'm not suggesting that isn't what happened, yet I would have expected by now to have received a report, especially under your current circumstances.

Further, you have a documented history of violence toward your children and now targeting a stepson, Thomas (Did you press charges against Thomas? If so, I would like to know that as well as it involves Junior). Junior being out of school for inclement weather this week means there was no check provided by his teachers.

Again, I'm not making an accusation. I am expecting on this occasion and on any similar occasion in future to receive a clear report of the incident. I would like to know the date, time, and location of the incident, the individuals involved and any adults involved directly or contacted thereafter, a summary of the incident, and the actions taken as a result of the incident – basically what one would summarize naturally following an incident of this nature. I would like this report today, February 1st.

This is another example of Junior not receiving the benefit of cooperative parenting. The parent acting as custodian —you — has the responsibility of updating the other parent concerning the child's wellbeing. Obviously, it can't work otherwise.

Thank-you for responding to this request,
Peter Walton"

THIRTY-SEVEN

Steven's Case is Moved to Florida and He Begins Again

"Evidence of parental alienation by a parent has been upheld by Florida appellate court as being sufficient to modify the parenting time in a divorce judgment. The bottom line is that parents that are able to put aside their animosity toward the other parent and put their child first will have an advantage in a contested Florida child custody case."
~*Howard Iken, Florida Attorney, Blog: The Law Firm of Ayo and Iken*

The state of Florida was ahead of the curve in recognizing PAS in hostile custody cases. So, in November of 2013 Steven agreed to move the custody case to Florida where Jo and the boys still lived. We carefully selected a very expensive, but highly recommended attorney, so we thought. At this time, Steven still needed representation in Alaska because of the NCIS investigation and because Jo was still fighting him over financial issues. Steven's attorney in Alaska had misrepresented him so egregiously he fired him and had hired a new attorney, even though that meant more retainer fees.

In May of 2014, nine months after returning to Virginia Beach, there was finally an opening for Steven at the Walter Reed National Military Medical Center (WRNMMC), for a month-long evaluation and intensive treatment before his retirement. He was working on SEAL Team IV with less responsibilities than he had ever before had in his military career. As his workload was winding down, the toll of the physical and mental injuries that he sustained during his career was winding up. He began to have severe night sweats and terrors, reliving firefights and other combat-related events on a nightly basis. It was so bad that I had to wake him up, sometimes three times a night, to change the bed and wipe him down, as the bedclothes were drenched up through the comforter and down to the mattress.

Professionals at the WRNMMC said that it would take at least fifteen years for the nightmares and combat consequences to his central nervous system to subside. They explained that he controlled his Amygdala (survival fight and flight response) during firefights and extremely dangerous situations so many times that the unnatural response would need to work its way out of his system—it didn't just go away, it was absorbed into his body.

Junior and I went with him because part of the program was to work with the families of these war heroes, to help us understand the challenges that we face in supporting them and to get support for our own unique challenges. When I was not in classes or going to appointments with Steven, I handled Steven's case in Alaska with his attorney there, Steven's case in Florida with his new attorney, and my case in Kentucky.

The attorney in Alaska needed information and documentation. Though the only issues yet to be resolved were financial, Jo continued to hurl additional accusations and "concerns" regarding Steven's visitations. Steven's attorney had been an Army JAG officer (she retired as a Colonel) and she was very easy to work with; it actually comforted me to talk and email with her because someone finally believed Steven and saw Jo for who she really was. She respected and understood Steven's career, his sacrifice and what was being taken from him. She represented Steven completely throughout the rest of the NCIS investigation so that he didn't have to be involved further. She assured us that though these types of investigations take time to resolve, he didn't need to worry about things turning against him again.

Steven paid a retainer to one of the leading PAS experts and another retainer to his attorney in Florida. The PAS expert explained that we needed another trial in order to bring all of the new information to the judge directly. To bring up all of the false allegations at one time—emphasizing Steven's career and accolades for twenty years, and our documentation of Jo—would be enough to turn the case. He recommended that Steven take the stand because his natural calm presents the opposite picture from how Jo portrays him. He could calmly explain himself, reveal the documented PAS and handle the cross-examination. If Jo was finally questioned in detail about her abuses and false allegations toward Steven—something that did not happen under the counsel of his first attorney—with expert testimony about her behavior, it would anger the judge because of her gross misuse of the legal system. The PAS expert had seen this happen in other cases with much less documentation. He would walk us through it.

Steven's attorney in Florida was abrasive, sure of himself, direct and intimidating, and had received accolades for his work in family court. Steven's first attorney, practicing in Anchorage, behaved as though he were intimidated by Jo and her attorney and seemed to believe her story—Steven constantly defended himself to this attorney. Jo went to consultations with all of the attorneys on the island so that Steven could not be represented in person, due to conflict of interest. She then hired the most accomplished and aggressive attorney on Kodiak; a Harvard graduate. This was his final case and he gave it all of his attention. For these reasons we thought that this time around, the opposite might work. With the help of the PAS expert and this aggressive attorney, we had hope.

I was still dealing with Peter's intrusive and abusive emails, his accusations against me and his demands about visitations. My therapist and the judge in my case determined that I suffered from Post-traumatic Stress Disorder (PTSD) from Peter's abuse. All of the then-current stressors were triggering stress from past events, especially because the original trauma was so fresh. Living with PTSD so acutely at this time, I re-experienced things that were similar to my experiences with Peter (e.g., a phrase, a tone of someone's voice, a smell, a certain behavior or personality trait), and I sometimes responded as if in a past traumatic event, in the present. Depending on the severity of the exposure, my response (even now) can appear as "over-reaction," "crazy" and "not based in reality," if an observer doesn't understand what's going on. Receiving messages from Peter was almost always a trigger because 1) he was trying to further traumatize me and, after twenty years of marriage, he knew what worked, and 2) he was my abuser, directly.

We had parent coordinators at this time. We had two because there can be no mediation when there is a perpetrator and a victim. We each had a parent coordinator to negotiate on our behalf.

This was all going on weeks before Steven's summer visitation. Jo had a brand-new audience.

Jo revved up her efforts in an attempt to prevent any visitation, and Steven's attorney turned out to be miserable to work with. He triggered me all the time with his accusations, questioning and demands, with no desire to understand or to go on the offensive to protect Steven. He didn't want to understand his career or his current situation in the intensive treatment program, so we were on the defensive again. It all began again, having to provide documentation to disprove Jo's false and outlandish accusations. This time, though, they included me and my case. I was defending myself in my own case and now in Steven's case, so the mental and emotional stress from exposure to traumatic reminders was doubled.

Thankfully Junior had activities and I had time off of work. I would sit in the family center, where there was internet, with Steven and my computers, preparing documents for the Florida attorney, sometimes for most of the day. We had made it clear to him that Steven could in no way deal directly with any of this—he needed to focus on his much-needed treatment, and I would only involve him if absolutely necessary. Despite this, the attorney repeatedly called and texted Steven questioning why I was so involved and demanding to talk to Steven directly. I was downright afraid of this attorney. At times, he reminded me of Peter; his demanding intrusions with expectations of immediate compliance were exhausting. I began to fall apart, emotionally and psychologically, under the weight of it all.

Of course, the professionals at WRNMMC were all involved in our chronic and acute situation. We could see the empathy in their eyes and they regularly expressed feelings of helplessness as they watched my and Steven's anguish, desperate for it to stop, day after day. While they tried to help Steven heal and to support our family, he and I were being attacked from many angles multiple times a day.

We went to marriage counseling as part of Steven's treatment program. After one session relaying the chaos surrounding the upcoming summer visit with Steven's boys, the counselor stopped us and said, "Steven you fucked up so badly by marrying your ex-wife that all ties need to be cut with your sons so you can be relieved of any communication from Jo. *It is critical for your health and not safe for Sabrina and Junior.* They are your family and you need to do what's best for them. Your boys are so badly damaged by their mother you cannot let that level of hate and violence in your home." All staff with whom he/we met with agreed and encouraged him to do this. Steven did not listen and this became a wedge between us. In his defense, and something I love about him, he has been trained to not give up on anything. He has an amazingly high threshold for adversity, which is why he tolerated Jo, along with her threats to take his boys from him.

A colleague of mine, a psychologist, with whom I shared this story, agreed that Junior and I were not safe, especially because he is younger than the two other boys. He relayed a personal story in his heartfelt explanation about how a family member had been a foster parent, with his wife, and had wanted to adopt a child that they were fostering; at the last minute, the mother fought for the child and won. Months later, she was addicted, and the boy was living on the streets—at a very young age. Years after this, the foster parents found the boy on the street and adopted him. They had children of their own by then. The boy, by then, was so badly damaged by being homeless for so long that he started to act out violently toward the biological children and his behavior could not be controlled. They put him back into the foster care system for the safety of their family. He saw similarities with Thomas and Jay's behavior, and in his professional opinion, strongly recommended that Steven not follow through with anymore visitation.

One evening, Steven and I went out. I felt unappreciated for handling everything with his ex-wife while he tried to have a summer visit with his boys, against professional opinion. I became very emotional and he was not in a position to handle it. We left the restaurant with me crying and hurting deeply. I was not at all stable, and was unable to handle all that was going on in his cases in addition to mine. Steven was unable to provide me with the love and comfort that I needed. I felt alone and emotionally attacked by Steven. And as it goes with PTSD, I reacted in a way that was detached from the current event and responded, instead, to my past with Peter. I ran away from Steven. It was night and, when I calmed down, I couldn't find my way back to the room at the house where we were staying. I was wearing wedge sandals and, in my haste, had sprained my ankle very badly, perhaps broken it. Now I was lying in front of a lit building crying about these new problems. Some employees were leaving late and found me; they took me to security, who got me back to the house. When I returned, Steven was sleeping, which triggered me again. I screamed at him and hit him in the chest.

The next day, the director of the treatment program interviewed Steven and me, separately, about the events of the previous night. Our stories were the same. The director was concerned as several couples staying in the same house had talked to her about my screaming and about security being in our room. Steven had been accused of domestic violence and I had an obvious injury. The director and some of the professionals that had been working with us then met with Steven and me together. Their response was incredible—they surrounded us with true empathy and no judgement. They made immediate arrangements for my treatment at the medical center, with no charge. Steven's team worked together to set up more appointments for me and more counseling for us together, and they followed up frequently with us after we left.

THIRTY-EIGHT

The Family that Stole Easter

Peter and Junior Skyped, often including Junior's sisters, about his upcoming spring break visitation to be with them in Canada. They did a ninety-day countdown and planned fun activities. They talked about seeing Peter's extended family and about how excited Junior's cousins were to see him. Steven and I planned a real honeymoon for the same week. I told Peter about our plans so that Steven and I could establish dates and book our trip. I believe that the following series of events happened to sabotage our plans.

The following email exchange is evidence that Peter knew the area for custody exchanges in Virginia Beach, where we lived, and had, in fact, already made an exchange at the same location during Thanksgiving break.

Email 11/22/2013

"Sabrina,

I want to follow up on the Thanksgiving break plan for Junior and provide you a financial update. Ms. G is available to meet me after Junior's school day on Tuesday. I simply would like an update from her on Junior's academic performance and encourage Junior by reaching out to his teacher.

Ideally, Junior could remain after school on Tuesday and I could begin caring for him at that time. I recognize that his school has a half-day on Wednesday. I would like to avoid leaving mid-day Wednesday in holiday traffic. By leaving Tuesday afternoon we can knock out a significant amount of the trip before stopping for night. Would you be willing to have Junior take his bag to school Tuesday and provide a signed note that communicates that you are aware Junior is travelling to Canada with me from the 26th thru December 1st? I am happy to have Junior call you before heading out Tuesday so you know I have arrived.

I was correct in saying a new banking system has been put in place in Canada which will more easily facilitate international transfers, but it is not implemented in the banks themselves. I learned today it will take "a few weeks." In the interim, I sent you 1.5 payments by regular mail directly to your Virginia Beach address (I hope you receive it tomorrow, or Monday-Tuesday). I will plan on sending an identical payment at the beginning of December. Please have your bank scan me a letter indicating that your name is on the bank account you indicated. If it is not, by chance, please provide banking information for a bank account in your name.

Thank-you for your consideration, and please respond at your earliest convenience.

Peter"

Email 11/22/2013
Re: Junior's Thanksgiving break (from me):
Peter,
Tuesday is fine, Junior and I talked about it and I was going to suggest that.
Will you take him to school on Monday Dec. 2nd? I will get you a bank account and that material. We are camping and possibly won't be home by 8:30 Sunday. You can call my phone Sunday. I would like to receive communication when Junior gets to Canada as well. The border crossing is anxiety provoking for him.

Peter had visitation with Junior during Christmas break—for the three days following our wedding. The next visitation was Easter Break. The following is the exchange leading up to the highly anticipated visitation. Our Parent Coordinators were copied on all email exchanges.

Email 4/4/2014

Subject: Re: Exchange plan

"Ms. Brown:

I am trying to determine when I can arrive to pick up Junior for his upcoming break. It's possible I can pick him up on the evening of the 11th - next Friday - but more likely on the afternoon of Saturday, April 12th. I can let you know as the week progresses. I would then plan on returning him on Sunday April 20th (Easter).

The plaza by Junior's school, where we did the exchange in the fall, would likely work well this time. Please provide a signed letter, with your contact information, describing the nature of the trip, for the Canadian/US Border Service; and Junior's allergy medication.

Thank-you,

Peter"

Email 4/6/2014

Subject: Re: Exchange plan

"Ms. Brown:

As you know, I am to Skype with Junior this evening, and I haven't received a reply to my email concerning spring break. Do you intend to support the trip by for example writing the letter for the border crossing, or, like last Easter, do you intend to intervene in some way to block interaction between Junior and me, and his sisters and extended family?

This would be helpful to know, considering the amount of preparation necessary to make a trip like this one. Would you consider providing an answer, perhaps for Junior's sake? It would be helpful to know your thinking before I speak with him this evening.

Thank-you for your consideration.

Peter"

Email 4/7/2014

Subject: Re: Exchange plan

"Ms. Brown:

I appreciate if you would clarify your intention to provide a signed note acknowledging Junior's travel with his father, for the US & Canadian Border Service. I can provide a more concrete time of arrival for Friday or Saturday as Friday progresses - April 11th.

Thank-you,
Peter"

Email 4/8/2014 (from me):

Subject: Re: Exchange plan

I've already confirmed this and will follow orders, that I established nearly a year ago.

April 12, 2014 at 02:19 PM:

Subject: Re: Exchange plan

"Ms. Brown:

Unfortunately, I couldn't get away until 2pm today, which means I will get down to your area too late for a Friday exchange. Can we tentatively plan on 10am in the morning - Saturday? (I'll sleep and be ready to roll).

Please let Junior know I'm disappointed I couldn't make it this evening, but I'm looking forward to the morning.

Thank-you, and I assume the plaza we did the exchange at last time works for you - plaza, 10am?

Peter"

April 12, 2014, at 4:08 AM:

Subject: Re: Exchange plan

"Update: I ran into spring break traffic, which slowed the trip considerably. I will likely be later than 10am. I can provide an update as I get into town.

Please acknowledge receipt of the email.

Thank-you,
Peter"

April 12, 2014 at 09:09 AM (from me):

Subject: Re: Exchange plan

I'm reasonably concerned about Junior's safety if you are planning to turn right around and drive again. Are you going to sleep somewhere before? I am flexible so that you can sleep or provide evidence that you won't drive all the way back with him today.

Apr 12, 2014, at 10:18 AM:

Subject: Re: Exchange plan

"Ms. Brown,

I understand completely on the sleep issue. I ended up stopping and was able to get sufficient sleep (i.e. as much as I usually get). I am quite close to the plaza now, and can meet you as soon as you are able.

Thank-you,
Peter"

April 12, 2014 10:58 AM:

Subject: Re: Exchange plan (from me):
11:30?

April 12, 2014, at 11:13 AM:

Subject: Re: Exchange plan
"Ms. Brown,
I am available whenever you are able to do the exchange.
Thank-you,
Peter"

April 12, 2014 at 11:42

Re: Exchange plan (from me):

We are in the parking lot in the truck.

April 12, 2014 at 11:59:20 AM
Subject: Re: Exchange plan
"I may be in the wrong plaza - hold on."

April 12, 2014 at 12:16 PM

Subject: Re: Exchange plan (from me):

I'm taking Junior back to the house to wait there and not in a vehicle. When you're at the right plaza let us know.

April 12, 2014 at 12:27 PM
Subject: Re: Exchange plan (from me):
You aren't here are you? I'm not interested in any games surrounding Junior and a border crossing. We have been extremely flexible being available for two days now. Junior is confused and we have no information for him. Be up front so I can have an accurate letter; it says YOU are taking him across the border. Junior already gets upset with the crossing. Please don't jeopardize timeshare for Junior's sake.

April 12, 2014 at 1:57 PM
Subject: Re: Exchange plan (from me):
Junior is very upset and rightly so. He has tried to call all of your numbers at least 4 times each and both of his sister's numbers. We are asking that you let us know what is going on. The plaza is the only plaza near Junior's school and a place you have been to already. If you are not here just let us know so that Junior isn't waiting for you not knowing how to handle what is going on.

April 13, 2014, at 10:09 AM (from me):
Parent Coordinator,
Peter has made no contact with Junior since 11:45 yesterday. He has been online and appears to be fine. Junior is extremely upset as he's been packed and expecting his dad since Friday. Yesterday he was worried something had happened and cried off and on all day. We are going to make other plans and we plan to ask for supervised time share in the U.S. going forward with the judge. This has been sheer craziness that no one can contact us.
Please intervene in any way you see will help, Sabrina

April 14, 2014 at 5:43 AM
"*Ms. Brown,*
Junior has reported during Skype sessions he is not permitted to view his email account, which his sister and I helped him set up at Thanksgiving. I

would like to ask that you begin allowing him to do so. Nothing prevents you from monitoring the account to assuage any concerns.

I have sent Junior a note to his email account, and I would like him to be free to read it.

Thank-you, Peter"

April 14, 2014 at 08:37 AM

"Did you and Peter finally facilitate Junior's exchange?

Thanks,
Parent Coordinator"

And another email:
"What was the explanation? This is very confusing to me too. I've sent him an email as well.
Thanks,
Parent Coordinator"

After the April fourteenth communication from Peter, I used social networking in an attempt to find out what happened. A mutual friend said that he was online, as were my girls, so they simply chose not to respond. My friend also warned me that Peter was likely setting me up to make claims that I prevented him from visitation, and she advised me to document the events.

This was devastating to Junior; he thought Peter was dead. I called jails and hospitals, to try and find out if he was okay. Luckily Steven and I had decided that we needed to save money and we never planned a vacation/honeymoon. Steven took the week off and I called the younger of my two brothers to see if he and his family could come for a visit—they came right away thankfully. Junior needed a distraction; he was beside himself with grief.

April 14, 2014 at 12:39 PM (from me):

Parent Coordinator,

He never came. You saw the emails all night and the statement he was close, etc. Junior left messages, he could barely speak he was crying. That was so bizarre and then to send that email 3 days later, apparently the explanation is in a 10-year old boy's email account that he was supposed to be checking? He couldn't answer his phone call?

This was the last visitation in our orders; he has not mentioned summer visitation at all. This last round of games leads me to fight for Junior to not leave this country. I won't stop him from seeing him, but I don't feel comfortable allowing Junior to go to Canada again. In the past I have felt comfortable because his sisters take great care of him, but with them not answering his phone calls as well fills me with grave concern for his well-being with the Walton family. My girls have not spoken to me now for over 4 years. We are moving back into the area at the end of the summer so I can come for meetings with you and bring Junior.

All the best, Sabrina

The following email came two days later in Junior's email account; this is how Peter let us know he was alive and well.

Email 4/16/ 2014

"Dear Junior,

I am so very proud of you, my one-and-only son, and I'm so very proud to be your one-and-only dad. We have a special connection!

I love you and miss you every single day. Every time I miss you I pray for you. I ask the Holy Spirit, who proceeds from the Father and the Son, to be present with you, to comfort you.

You know from the Nicene Creed that the Holy Spirit is the Giver of Life. He's the glue that binds together the Father to the Son, and the Son to the Father. That's why I ask the Holy Spirit to bind us together - father and son, son and father. That's what He specializes in!

I so much look forward to spending time with you. It is such a pleasure to be around you. You are always welcome with me.

Take good care,

Dad"

Junior and I had shopped together for his sisters. We had put together Easter baskets for them and we had ordered extra school pictures that year for whomever wanted them in the Walton family.

Email 4/20/2014

"*Ms. Brown:*

I look forward to speaking with Junior this evening on Skype. Please let me know of any change to the 8:30pm Skype time (I want to make sure I'm at a computer at the right time).

If for whatever reason a Skype session won't work this evening, I would appreciate the opportunity to speak with Junior over the phone. Will you make an exception to your no phone contact rule? Please let me know.

Thank-you,

Peter"

I forwarded that email to the parent coordinators with this message:

Email 4/20/2014

Happy Easter,

Junior deserves an explanation for the extremely bizarre experience he has been forced to deal with. We can then process it with his therapist here in Virginia Beach before any interaction with Peter. He has finally stabilized from the blow, brushing over all of this would be detrimental to his mental state. This is the first time he has tried to make contact with Junior since his goodbye email [email April 16, above] so this all seems to be a psychological game with a 10-year-old.

As always, your intervention in this matter is much appreciated!

Sabrina

Email 5/7/2014

"*Ms. Brown:*

I continue to wait for word from you concerning contact with my son.

Junior has enjoyed very limited, controlled contact with me under your Soviet-like custodianship since April 2012 when I moved to Ontario to in large part escape your escalating attacks (despite the considerable distance you've made two aggressive attempts to have me arrested, and you've succeeded in having your new stepson arrested in the witching hours of January 1st 2014 – and your year began).

Now you've removed even the twice-weekly Skype sessions – this despite the fact you and I were ordered on more than one occasion in Family Court to co-parent. Far from co-parenting, the assault on me, your own daughters, my extended family, and others has continued, and even increased in intensity. Your libellous attack blog is more than two-years old with over 50,000 hits. You have failed to counter the multiple death threats and threats of violence to my person received over your Facebook account (these are forwarded to me from some of our former mutual friends). Your daughters are subjected to humiliation after humiliation at your hand.

Your email of April 20th to our parent coordinators, which I too was included in, suggests Junior will need to process missing me over his spring break with a therapist before he can have contact with me. You report concern for his mental state. Have you considered yet what it does to a boy to be ripped away from his father and his siblings? It's necessary for you to try and defame me, and a growing list of others, in order for your campaign to maintain any momentum. Tragically, Junior is the casualty of your unrelenting cruelty.

I last had contact with Junior in mid-April. Will you commit to resuming Skype-sessions and allowing me unlimited phone contact (within reason, of course), and will you commit to supporting Junior in spending his entire summer in Ottawa with me and his sisters? (Consider what you are doing to Junior in blocking his interaction with his sisters who adore him). I am eager to care for Junior throughout the summer, beginning on Saturday June 14.

I'm ready for a phone call or Skype session with Junior as soon as possible. Please let me know.

Thank-you, Peter"

Email 5/18/2014

"Ms. Brown:

I have again tried calling Junior this evening twice, but you are not answering. I called so I could speak to my son for a few minutes. It's been well over a month now since I have spoken to Junior. Will you permit a phone call so I might say hello? I miss my son. I have also tried to get on Skype, but there was no response on your end.

Apparently you are convincing yourself it is the right thing to alienate my son from me, as you have done before for periods of time. Have you considered you may not be right, that Junior may be concerned about his sisters and me? Are you concerned Junior may be in an environment where he is not free to express himself, and so he keeps his real feelings locked away? Weren't you raised in a similar, highly constricted environment?

It's clear you lack the confidence to allow Junior to have a relationship with me, free of your coercion? The problem is that perspective keeps the focus on you and your discomfort. This isn't about you. You have a relationship with Junior, and I deserve to have a relationship with Junior as well. Will you consider discontinuing your hate campaign against me and allowing me to cultivate a relationship with Junior? Even further, why wouldn't you encourage the relationship?

I would appreciate you thinking more broadly about this issue. I'll keep appealing to reason. It is odd, though not as much today with the dumbing down of the academy, that you are a university professor unwilling to look at an issue objectively.

Thank-you for your consideration. I hope at some point you would welcome an opportunity to live life free of courts and litigation, and accusation - because Junior is in your care at this time. Is this how you want him to remember this period of his life? Or, are you even considering such things?

Peter"

Email 5/25/2014

"Ms. Brown:

I called your number just a few minutes ago to try to reach Junior. Another week has gone by and I continue to be alienated from my son - zero contact.

On what is likely a related matter, I have been waiting for you to cash the child support cheque I sent for Junior. Are you holding onto the cheque? Are you concerned that accepting child support from me diminishes your whole "I Married a Sociopath" blog/book campaign? That is, if you accept the cash at this point, how do you continue to justify alienating me from my son.

...The other rationale for cutting off my contact with Junior is to promote *your move toward eliminating my parental rights so that, as you put it in an email (though it was to look as if Steve Brown wrote it), your brand new husband could adopt Junior.*

...both you and your new husband also deal with dependency issues, likely related in large part to numbing the effects of trauma; your collective histories of child rearing leave a great deal to be concerned about (on Tuesday May 27th, Junior has a formal review to discuss his excessive absences at now a second school - more than 50 full day absences this school year and last combined)..."

Upon arriving in Virginia Beach and signing Junior up at a new school I had asked for a meeting with the school counselor. I talked with her about my situation with Peter and my concern for Junior's wellbeing in all of it. I asked that she meet with him regularly so that he had someone to talk to about everything that was going on with him.

I also met with the Principal of the school to let her know of my difficulties with Peter surrounding communication and timeshare with Junior and how unpredictable Peter could be. I also explained how Peter had used Junior's prior school systems, and Principals, to try and control me and/or disparage me and he would likely do that again with her, here.

Junior did miss a lot of school that year. He started late and we lived with Steven for part of his month-long treatment program at the WRNMMC. It was recommended that, if possible, the entire family participate. I always kept the school informed and got as much schoolwork ahead of time as possible. He was doing exceptionally well academically so there were no red flags with the school.

Peter was calling in on the twenty-seventh (less than a month before the end of the school year) and had asked for not only that school's administrators to all be present, but for district representation. When she and I talked, she told me that they were planning on meeting with me and Steven later, but Peter insisted that I be present when he called in.

On the twenty-seventh, Steven and I arrived with the court order that Peter and I have no verbal communication. The order was a result of me dropping the Emergency Protective Order against Peter. They passed it around and decided that I could not be present in the room when Peter called and they would meet with us after, as planned.

When they asked us into the room following Peter's call, I could tell by the looks on their faces what had happened. The Principal said that they understood why I had the order and the call had not gone well after they told him about the court order and me not being present. He did not have nice things to say about me.

Email 5/25/2014 (continued)

"...*and Junior's natural wishes for maintaining the security of his relationship with me, a loving father, are stifled*

Again, I am asking that you permit contact between Junior and me. I ask you do so as soon as is possible for Junior's sake. He in no way deserves your punishment.

I will try calling again in a few minutes.

Thank-you,

Peter"

This time Steven responded:

Email 5/25/2014

"*Peter,*

Steve Brown, Dr. Browns husband, just wanting to clarify that I did write about adopting Junior. He is a terrific son that I very much enjoy fathering. I'm glad my job allowed me to drop everything over Easter break to help him recover from the huge blow of not traveling to Canada. He was very excited to make the trip and had expressed his feelings to his friends, teachers and coaches, Junior was terribly embarrassed having not gone. He and I went to mass on Palm Sunday and were able to spend some quality time together at home and even at my command. Maybe setting Junior up with airline travel would be a better mode of travel for the future. Junior is growing into a fine young man and deserves an explanation of what happened over this past Easter, I am more than willing to facilitate building back trust between you and Junior...all of us have his best interest in mind. As for your check, Dr. Brown has not received one, I believe it has been requested that a regularly scheduled transfer or direct deposit be established between you and her, that would elevate any international mailing issues. I use a government service to ensure the child support I provide for my children is received on time and in full, maybe this could be another option to help Junior....

Regards. Steve."

Email 5/28/2014

"Hey Peter,

I have recently been informed that you may think that Dr. Brown kept Junior from you for the Easter visit. I can positively say that is not the case as I was with the two of them waiting in the parking lot of the designated strip mall for Junior's exchange. Father to Father I understand the importance of relationships between our sons. As I suggested in an earlier email maybe an airline ticket could resolve any possible interference of visitation. I sent an email to you earlier but not sure if you received it since there has been no response. I look forward to helping your relationship with Junior, he is really growing into an awesome man. Regards. Steve."

Email 6/2/2014

"Ms. Brown:

I tried calling Junior again yesterday and you didn't answer or have Junior return my call. It is now approaching two months since you blocked me from interaction with my son. This is the same behaviour you exhibited one year ago. On what basis could you justify interrupting my relationship with my son? I would ask again that you permit contact between Junior and me. Will you now consider mitigating the damage you are doing to Junior - your own son - and indirectly to your daughters? He doesn't deserve your punishment. He's done nothing wrong. I understand it must be incredibly threatening for you to consider releasing Junior - imagine if he were permitted to peer over the walls you've constructed.

On another note, I sent you a child support check weeks ago and it has not been cashed. Setting up a new banking arrangement, as I've explained *previously, was incredibly difficult. Would you like to explain why you are not accepting the cash? Are you wanting me to cancel the check I sent? I don't understand.*

Finally, I have not received any confirmation from you regarding the gifts my parents have been sending Junior. Is he receiving them, or are you throwing them out? As I've stated before, even prisoners are permitted to receive mail. What is your explanation for cutting off Junior's grandparents? Are you actually going to force my parents to appear in a Virginia Beach court in order to work out an arrangement for spending time with their grandson? Would this expenditure of time and money on the part of my parents be gratifying for you in some way? Would it be akin to your disparaging of my parents on your blog? I believe they would articulate well in court their suffering as a result of your alienating Junior from them.

As I've been saying for years now, all it takes for communication to improve/begin is for you to make a conscious decision to pivot. I would like Junior here for a significant party that is occurring in our family in late June. Please respond to the proposal I have made previously for the exchange.

Thank-you for your consideration,
Peter"

Steven responded:

Email 6/2/2014

"Hey Peter,

Junior deserves an explanation why you abandoned him on Easter break. To play him like a pawn is very damaging to the growth of a young man. We will continue to protect Junior until you can man up and just tell him why…

…no check has ever been received…Junior has been receiving gifts from his Grandparents. The last being brain quest cards.

If there are any questions feel free to contact me. Regards. Steve."

Email 6/10/2014

"Peter,

Junior would like to Skype tonight at the usual time. Sabrina and Junior had a discussion about seeing you and Junior is still very concerned with and would like to know what happened to his trip over Easter break. If you are willing to talk to Junior let us know, if we don't receive a reply we will take that as a "no". Be honest to Junior, I have heard your reason, to people, over Easter, why Junior was not in Canada was we didn't allow him to go, and you had to drive all the way to Virginia for not. Also, why his sisters and you wouldn't take phone calls or return his calls over a three day period. Junior was in our vehicle at the right place at the right time for his exchange when you told us that you were at the wrong location and on your way to the right location. Regards. Steve."

Email 6/12/2014

"Ms. Brown:

Last evening you permitted Junior to interact with me over Skype. Despite all of my requests, it was the first interaction in two months. And, despite your shadow hovering over the screen, Junior began to let down and enjoyed the interaction with me and with his sister. She was very excited to know she would be able to see her brother yesterday. Junior clearly looks up to both of his sisters.

After about 7 minutes, you entering the screen and making demands on how I should proceed on the Skype session with my son, yelling that your daughters are "half you," and that I reject both "biology and genetics," in regard to your decision to avoid any attempt at contact with your daughters - for more than two years now -was highly unfortunate, especially for Junior and his sister. I can't imagine how awful Junior must feel. Yelling that I am a "sociopath" was simply more damage done.

I was unable to convince you to allow me to have time with my son alone over Skype and you shut us down, briefly allowed the session to begin again when I dialed back, and almost immediately shut us down again.

What I continue to ask for is cooperation from you in allowing me time with my son. That episode was highly, highly unfortunate. Please consider that our only interaction now is to revolve around Junior, nothing more.

Peter"

Email 6/12/2014 (from me):

Peter,

It is very unfortunate that you chose to trick and deceive Steve, me and Junior over spring break. It is unfortunate that Junior cannot leave this country *because of you and his sisters not answering his call for three days following, and giving us, now months later, still no explanation. It is unfortunate that Skype was used to message me, talk about a summer trip and activities to Canada and shame about him not Skyping. Following Skype Junior and I re-read all of your emails from spring break and I explained that this was not his fault or mine, and he understands that you will never tell him the truth and he understands why it is unsafe for him go to Canada under your care. It is unfortunate that a 10-year-old boy has to deal with such heart break. What would have been really great for Junior is for you and the girls to pick him up, or fly him up to Canada, over his spring break and be a man of character and your word. We would be having an entirely different conversation about summer visitation if spring break had been handled as it was planned and ordered. I am disappointed in all of you hurting an innocent child. There will be no more Skype until all of this is resolved.*

THIRTY-NINE

The Living Death

Junior's sisters are so much older than him that they are like second moms. During and after my horrible, unnecessarily hostile and highly litigated divorce from Peter, his sisters chose only to interact with their brother during Peter's court ordered time-share. Peter controlled all communication between them and Junior. In an age where communication is so easy his sisters elected to not independently communicate with their little brother. He missed them terribly; they were his heroes and stars. He went to so many ballet and singing lessons, why wouldn't he think the world of them? When I took the girls to their lessons, I usually brought Junior with us. We watched the girls together.

Junior was very sad about everyone moving to Canada. He talked about his sisters a lot. Skype sessions, after they moved to Canada, revolved around Junior visiting them, not them visiting him, not them asking about his life, what he wanted, what mattered to him, only anticipation of his visits to them. He was so excited about the spring break vacation with his sisters, cousins and dad. At that time, I encouraged the relationship between Peter and Junior, so I also talked about the trip with Junior and got excited about it. We decided to get Easter gifts for his sisters, so we went to the store and bought a musical note pin for the opera singer, a peacock pin for the dancer, a rock that read "love," a rock that read "faith," candles, Easter bunnies, cards and baskets in which to put all of the gifts.

When no one showed up, Junior's pain was the worst that I have ever seen or heard from any of my children. He was inconsolable. And he called them and left messages in that pain, they had to hear it. He could barely talk he was crying so hard. He was asking for his dad, asking if he was dead—he was in anguish. No one answered. No one explained and no one apologized.

He was just a little boy; he had no control. I had no control. I couldn't help him feel better. Steven tried to help him feel better. He had no control over when or even if he would ever see his sisters again.

He had two sisters and then he had none.

FORTY

First, Do No Harm

"The Court has no doubt that the cause of the blind, brainwashed, bigoted, belligerence of the children toward the father grew from the soil nurtured, watered and tilled by the mother. The Court is thoroughly convinced that the mother breached every duty she owed as the custodial parent to the noncustodial parent of instilling love, respect and feeling in the children for their father. Worse, she slowly dripped poison into the minds of these children, maybe even beyond the power of this Court to find the antidote."
~Schutz v. Schutz (Judge Opinion)

In 1997, based upon the above quote and what he was observing in his own cases, Judge Nakahara, a family court judge in California, cautioned family law judges to be aware that in addition to the child, professionals upon whom the court relies may also be "brainwashed" by the alienating parent. This includes attorneys, family court services and private counselors. The opinions of various professionals who become involved should not be accepted as authoritative simply because individuals designated as professionals are making them. The opinions of professionals need to be tested and critically evaluated by the court.

Attorneys and parents must also be held accountable. During his term on the family law bench,

Judge Nakahara did not allow the common family law practice of the court relying on attorneys' representations as to what their client, parents and other witnesses would testify to if called. Similar to criminal cases, he insisted on live testimony so that he could test the credibility of witnesses himself.

At first, family lawyers in his courtroom were surprised that he expected them to show substantial proof in support of their claims and of their client's position. They were also surprised by his readiness to impose sanctions. Attorneys quickly learned that they needed to be more careful about their representations in Judge Nakahara's court room and that they would be required to back up their claims.

According to Judge Nakahara, holding parents accountable builds success. Relieving a parent of sanctions builds failure and increases the likelihood that unacceptable behavior will recur. Failure to impose sanctions when sanctions are called for reinforces parents' disregard for court orders and their belief that they can do as they please [6].

Steven's Florida attorney had all of this information at his disposal and had spent a career in family law. Additionally, there were ample red flags of PAS dating all the way back to the *Findings of Fact and Conclusions of Law* from Steven and Jo's divorce in October of 2011—the document upon which the present mediation was based. For example, "There is no doubt in the court's mind that Mr. Brown is both willing and able to allow the children to have meaningful relations with their mother. The court is a little concerned that Mrs. Brown has been not completely willing and able to allow the children to have a meaningful relationship with their father... The court finds that the children want to be with their father; they miss him; they haven't had any real, meaningful, sustained visits with their father since they left Kodiak. It is important for their overall development." And later in October 2013, right before the custody case was moved to Florida, "as the court has long been concerned with Jo's (in)ability to let the boys have a meaningful relationship with their father."

I provided to Steven's attorney more-than-sufficient documentation through emails and police reports from false allegations. I set up phone interviews for him with Dr. Michael Bone (the PAS expert whom we had retained and who lived close to the law firm's office) and eyewitnesses—he declined the interviews and gave no regard to all that I had prepared. He did not include any documentation in response to Jo's attorney's claims. He contended that he and Jo's attorney would work for the best interest of the children, yet he did not act on Steven's emails asking for him to consider PAS.

> Email 3/ 26/2014
> *Attorney CB,*
> *This was the second interaction with my sons since 1/5/14. This was the same as the first so we decided to video thinking it would happen again. If I do have rights as their father, I would like to take action as soon as possible. Please initiate whatever you can so I can have meaningful interactions with my sons. You have seen the pictures of them without the influence of their mother; this video is obviously the result of parent alienation syndrome. I appreciate your urgency in this matter.*
> *Regards,*
> *Steve"*

Steven's attorney called him immediately only to shame Steven for recording a Skype session during which his boys came on the screen only to say, "I have nothing to say to you," and then hung up. There was no concern over what was happening to the boys, only that Steven had recorded the Skype session. Neither Steven's first attorney nor this attorney interviewed collaterals, polygraphed (or even questioned) Jo regarding her allegations or recommended a full psychological evaluation of the family.

Dr. J. Michael Bone and Michael R. Walsh:

"Make no mistake about it. Individuals with either PAS or a related malicious syndrome will and do lie! They are convincing witnesses, and their manipulative skills may influence others to follow suit [22]."

Steven spent approximately thirty-thousand dollars trying to have summer visitation in 2014 with his boys, as ordered. He was spending time and money defending himself against false allegations.

He had gone out on his own for a while after the thousands he spent on both attorneys for the last summer visitation. He had spent even more just trying to get the boys to our December wedding and visitation.

During the time that Steven self-represented, Jo and her attorney actively made accusations about Steven and me, trying to prevent visitation based on these false narratives. For example, on one occasion, Steven took Jay to an upstairs room to talk to him privately. Before the next visitation, Steven was accused of interrogating Jay and forcing him to say negative things about Jo at gun point. In reality, he stored unloaded guns in locked *Pelican* cases along with some compound hunting bows in this room. He did not even consider this; his only intention was to have a private conversation with his son.

When Steven was changing his child support payments into a new system in Florida, the payments weren't going through correctly, but because Steven had set them up as automatic, he didn't check if they were actually going through. After a few months, without any notification, Jo's attorney threatened that Steven needed to appear in court in three days, in Florida, or there would be a warrant out for his arrest. He paid the back-due support and the issue was dropped. Three more times, she made this threat. The third time, Steven and I decided to go to court and use the opportunity to open things up in front of the judge, as the PAS expert had recommended.

Wanting to really open things up Steven contacted his attorney in Florida and told him about our plans, then we began the trip to Florida. Instead of representing Steven and his wishes, the attorney fought with him (at $350 an hour) all the way to Georgia where we stopped overnight. All along he didn't believe that we were actually coming. Apparently, it was common practice for this attorney to threaten court appearances but never actually follow through. When they spoke, while we were in Georgia, Steven had to convince him that we were still on our way. It was during this conversation his attorney refused to prepare to go to court, saying that he had always mediated, instead—this judge wouldn't like it and would not act favorably toward Steven because of it. Steven's attorney's reputation was more important to him than helping Steven. We turned around and went back home.

By this time, Steven had received his disability rating from the U.S. Department of Veteran Affairs; he was given a 100% combat-related disability rating. When a rating is assigned prior to divorce, the money is not considered in any calculations for child support. If a rating is given after divorce, it is up to the judge. Steven's attorney included, without question or concern, Steven's hard-earned disability pay as income in his child support calculation. Steven argued that he was unable to work at this time and that disability was his only income; his attorney argued back that he had my income, that he had a lot of equity in the two houses and that he had the rest of his disability. He also concluded—based on Jo's attorney's comments that Steven could earn a great deal of money in private industry given his experience as a Navy SEAL—that Steven should have no problem earning through employment. This all came after Steven's attorney flippantly commented that no judge would appreciate Jo's lack of employment or her use of Steven's child support as income.

During the final mediation, Steven's attorney argued that my blog was preventing co-parenting; he said to Steven that he was disgusted with what he read and shamed both Steven and me. He said that co-parenting could not occur until my blog was taken down. The attorney did not consider Jo's part in the deterioration of Steven's relationship to the boys and he and Jo's attorney agreed upon parameters for the mediation with the united presumption that I was the problem.

Steven's first Alaska attorney aided in solidifying and perpetuating a false domestic violence abuse allegation; now, his Florida attorney was participating in PAS, thereby increasing the severity of PAS symptoms in Steven's boys. Both attorneys 1) lacked competence, 2) did not follow Steven's instructions, and 3) there were ethical concerns regarding their communication with both Steven and me.

FORTY-ONE

Summer Visitation, 2014

"The advent of a new partner in divorce may escalate parental disputes over the child or precipitate new ones. A parent who feels threatened by an ex-spouse's new partner may initiate efforts to gain increased control of custody and visitation."

~Dr. J.L. Johnston and Dr. L.E. Campbell, *Impasses of Divorce: The Dynamics and Resolution of Family Conflict*

Email 5/16/2014

"*Ms. Brown:*

You have now blocked Junior from contact with me and his sisters for over one month. I can't conceive how you would construe alienating Junior from most of his family, simply because you are currently in a position to do so, as a healthy decision for Junior. It certainly is not.

I would ask you to let me know when Junior can call me or I can call him. I sincerely hope you recognize your intentional alienation of Junior from me and me from Junior. I hope no one injures Junior emotionally (and I pray not physically or sexually, as has long been the case in your incestuous family system) - one more injurious decision against your children...."

After I received this email, I did something that I would learn later was very important in protecting Steven, Junior and me; I called the state social services department.

I explained that Steven and I had both gone through hostile divorces and that both of our ex-spouses had made many false allegations. I explained that Steven's sons were coming for the summer and that I expected the allegations to resume. The intake social worker assured me that she would flag all of our names in the system and that, if they received a call, the information that I had given would be considered.

Jo was still preventing visitation and refused to put the boys on the flight for which Steven had already purchased tickets. Steven's attorney, instead of pushing for her to abide by orders and relaying that she would be in contempt of court if she did not put them on the plane, simply told Steven that it wasn't going to happen—she was refusing—and that he would have to drive to Florida to pick up the boys. During mediation, Jo insisted that the boys were so angry with me that they needed two weeks alone with Steven (without me and Junior).

We were only in Virginia Beach until Steven's retirement, July 2014, then we planned to sell the house and move back to Kentucky for my work. We purchased a campground which we thought would be a perfect setting in which Steven could bond with the boys.

Steven plans to use his training to teach and mentor young fatherless boys. He will provide instruction in survival/primitive living, land navigation—with compass and maps, the use and care of modern camping/backpacking equipment and outdoor clothing systems. Why not start with his own boys? We believed this to be the perfect place to heal their broken hearts, feel the love of our family, appreciate all that their dad had to offer them—all without the interruption or distraction of electronics. For these reasons we did not fight Jo's demand that the boys have two weeks alone with Steven, though it was strange that suddenly I was the sole problem while Steven was now a good dad.

FORTY-TWO

The Sexual Abuse Allegation

"In PAS with false allegations of abuse, the child is also corrupted by repeated involvement in discussions of deviant sexuality regarding the target parent or other family and friends associated with that parent. In some cases of severe PAS, the alienating parent trains the child to be an agent of aggression against the target parent, with the child actively participating in deceits and manipulations for the purpose of harassing and persecuting the target parent."
~Dr. Deirdre Rand (Dr. Ira Daniel Turket), Child visitation interference in divorce

A false sexual accusation against me, involving Steven's boys, would further a number of Jo's strategies. First, it would put a permanent wedge between me and the boys. Second, Steven would have difficulty defending the accusations because they were not directed against him. Third, it could create conflict between Steven and me. Lastly, and most importantly, it would be the perfect way to extract Junior and me from Steven's life, and to align Steven with her agenda [17].

Three days before Steven was supposed to pick up the boys for summer visitation, Thomas made a false sexual abuse allegation against me to his therapist. Ironically he made the allegation during the court-ordered anger management therapy because he choked Junior.

Steven's attorney called to relay the accusation, minimizing the huge impact that it carried, and said that it was just a teenage boy who was mad about having to visit for the summer. The attorney assured Steven that it wouldn't take too long to clear up the situation —everyone involved saw what was going on. All that he could tell us was that the event was alleged to have happened three days after we married, in December 2013, and that a detective in Virginia Beach would call him soon.

Jo called Steven, left voicemail messages and sent text messages attempting to promote this false allegation and stating that they needed to work together to protect their son against me. When Steven picked up the boys, she walked toward him in an attempt to converse about the false allegation—again arguing that they needed to work together to protect their son against me.

Though Steven and the boys had not had a real conversation for months. They had only come on to Skype to say, "I have nothing to say to you," and though Thomas had just made a sexual allegation against me, the boys acted as though nothing had happened and they were all over him with affection. Steven's boys got into *my* car, that Steven drove, and immediately fell asleep. They slept for most of the first thirty-six hours with Steven. They appeared to be exhausted, likely from the months of alienation from him and seemed to be content to just be with him.

When the detective called Steven, he was so upset that he had to pull the car over; his threshold was crossed. The detective immediately asked, "Do you think that your wife would do something like this?" He responded, "No way." He explained the nature of the divorce and the other false allegations from Jo and the boys. She believed him.

She went on to tell him about the accusation. Allegedly, three days after our wedding, when Thomas was fifteen, I entered his bedroom while, the boys were visiting us during Christmas break. Thomas claimed that I forced him to touch me and that I said that, if he told anyone, I would do the same to his younger brother. He claimed to have been afraid to tell anyone.

During the boys' visit with Steven, I was at a work conference. I took Junior with me because Steven was unable to watch him while he was gone with his boys. A former employee (turned friend) was with me, thank goodness. Steven, still at the side of the road, short of breath, his voice shaking slowly started telling me what I was accused of, knowing how much it would hurt me. He started to tell me the accusation, and I had to hang up in order to find a garbage can in which to throw up. I called him back and he finished relaying the crushing information. I was in a daze, wandering around the city, with my friend and son, trying to make it through just each next minute without falling apart. Steven explained that the detective was on my side and saw through the allegation. Even so, the police had to conduct a full investigation. Steven was on his way to Kentucky to spend two weeks away from me and with my accuser. These two weeks were a blur—the worst days of my life. I could feel myself starting to lose my mind.

Steven gave his undivided attention to the boys. They did all of the outdoor activities that Steven had planned, and he talked a lot with them about truth, finding their truth and the importance of a man's word.

FORTY-THREE

Steven Retires

*"In Munchausen syndrome by proxy involving older children, it is the parent who originally initiated the child's factitious illness or victimization. In the context of a continued symbiotic parent / child relationship, older children may then learn to set up this situation themselves, producing factitious symptoms which induce a complicitous response from the MSP parent. Similarly, in moderate to severe **PAS**, children may learn to get their needs met by fabrication and manipulation."*

~Dr. Deirdre Conway Rand, Muchausen Syndrome by Proxy: A Complex type of Emotional Abuse Responsible for some False Allegations of Child Abuse in Divorce

I wanted to celebrate Steven's incredible career with a retirement party, while he wanted to slip out quietly with no pomp and circumstance. I insisted that we have a full military retirement ceremony on base at the SEAL Heritage Center, but in the end, we compromised and decided to host the celebration in our back-yard, which was large and beautiful. Considering all that had been going on with Peter, Jo, and the attorneys, Steven's treatment program, the move, the wedding, childcare, and traveling back and forth between

Kentucky and Virginia Beach all year, I did not have much time to plan the event. I was counting on these few summer weeks off of work to finalize arrangements. We invited members of his Team, neighbors and friends in the area, our families, and Steven's closest friends and "brothers" who lived in other parts of the country. I couldn't cancel; people had already bought plane tickets and made various reservations.

I was teaching a course and returned to Kentucky for a couple of intensive classroom days. I could conduct the remainder of the class on-line from Virginia Beach.

After the two-week period, Junior and I met Steven and his boys at the camp. My best friend stayed with us those first couple of nights to be a witness for me. In the morning, as she and I both prepared to leave for work, we walked into the living room where Thomas and Jay were sleeping. The boys were clutching each other as a married couple would. My friend and I looked at each other in astonishment and both thought that it was very odd behavior. Jo insisted that the boys sleep together while at our house (extremely odd for being fifteen-and twelve-year-old brothers). Though they started out in separate beds at Steven's insistence, throughout the visitation they often ended up sleeping together in this manner.

We all returned to Virginia Beach days before the retirement party, and the investigation began immediately. Thomas and Jay were interviewed first. Jay made several sexual allegations against me, as well (e.g., Jay claimed that I forced them to watch pornography and then talked about it with them afterwards). They looked detectives and social workers in the eye and coldly, without conscience, lied.

I was interrogated for hours the day before Steven's retirement celebration. The detective seemed to believe me and support me, Steven had this same feeling from the detective, as well. The social worker, however, did not appear to believe me. I had to sign a form vowing that I would not be alone with Thomas until the investigation concluded. I was placed on a registry for one year during which, if anything else happened, I would be arrested.

I told the detective that I believed that both boys were being sexually abused, though not in our home. I went on to tell the detective that I had thought this the first time that I saw them sleep together and observed their sexualized behaviors. This proved to be an important statement when the detective returned to our home about a real sexual abuse charge.

After learning of all that Thomas and Jay had told to police, including Thomas' statement saying he had NOT choked Junior and was, instead, the victim in that case, I couldn't even look at Thomas. I was never alone with him. He should *never have come into our home again*, and both Steven and I regret that he did.

FORTY-FOUR

The Retirement Party

I had no business hosting Steven's retirement party. I was shut down and broken. His dad and stepmother arrived the night before the celebration, while his mother stayed with us as another adult witness until the investigation was over. My family stayed at a hotel and took charge of Junior. We picked up one of Steven's closest friends, Todd and Todd's wife (Jane) at the airport—they were arriving from California. Steven and I had attended their wedding early on in our relationship. Everyone took care of food and helped me to get ready. Everything was last minute.

Those that came from Steven's command had no idea what was going on, so the ceremony turned out to be a very meaningful event for Steven.

My dad had just had surgery for a pacemaker, and we were still concerned about his heart. He and my mom were devastated about what was transpiring. My dad pulled me aside and said that Thomas and Jay had been on their phone with Jo the entire day telling her everything that was going on. He said, his face white and with great despair, "You can't live like this, it's not possible, it's too much." Steven's dad, stepmother and mom were hovering around Thomas and Jay showing their support to them.

Steven had known Todd's wife, Jane, prior to meeting me, and had spent some time at their house. When they heard of our crisis, she was very sympathetic toward Steven and me. As the day progressed, and alcohol was introduced, she involved herself in our crisis disregarding appropriate boundaries. I occasionally looked for Steven and saw them huddled in a quiet space as she affectionately checked in on how he was. She also became very affectionate toward his boys, checking in with them as well. At one point, I was sitting next to her husband and I asked him how he handled her flirtatiousness. He responded that it's easier to just let her go and not fight it—it didn't bother him.

At another point during the afternoon Jane approached Steven and said that she had a headache. He made coffee for her, got her his own prescribed medication (and gave her all that he had), then sat with her in the kitchen until her headache subsided. Steven was taking care of Jane and her needs while I was suffering so deeply, I didn't know how to function—I was in a daze, wandering around not knowing how to settle myself and be okay.

As evening approached and people started leaving—my parents had already taken Junior back to their hotel—Jane started to wrestle with Steven's boys and Steven joined in. They were all laughing and having a great time rolling around together. I had to leave the room. For hours, she interjected herself into a position that was not legally available to me. This day was supposed to be a celebration of Steven with me, his wife, at his side.

Because of the seriousness of Thomas's accusation, the detective suggested I not stay overnight in the same house as Thomas. As it turned out, our neighbors were gone so Steven and I stayed there along with Todd and Jane. I finally convinced Steven to leave the boys and to go next door. Exhausted, I wanted to go to bed, and so did his friend. Jane and Steven wanted to go for a swim in our backyard pool. I didn't want to leave them alone while Steven was in a vulnerable state, so we all went swimming together. No one had brought towels, so Steven went into our house to retrieve some for each of us. He didn't come out. Todd and Jane said to leave him, that he probably wanted to stay with his boys. He had been drinking which was one of Jo's primary accusations against Steven's parenting. I went into the house and found him lying on the floor where the boys were sleeping. I was concerned that when they woke, they would see that he had been drinking and passed out and would relay this to Jo. I should've just left him, but I was not thinking straight. I was utterly afraid of Jo and of what she might do next. I had been interrogated fewer than twelve hours earlier. I tried to shake Steven and I yelled at him to wake up. In a full panic, I slapped him across the face to wake him up. He awoke and said that he was staying at the house, and "I choose my boys." I went over the edge. I screamed at the boys, "You ruined my life you little fuckers!" Many times, I had come to the edge of what I felt in this moment, but this time I lost control of my mind.

I don't remember much else from that night, but during the years since, I have put the pieces together. I became hysterical and tried to run away. Steven and I went to the other house and fought hard. Todd had to get involved; Jane had passed out. Then I went back to our house to pack and leave, but Steven's mother held me while I cried uncontrollably. At some point, I went back to the house next door, and Steven and I fell asleep holding each other. We slept until five o'clock in the evening. When we woke up, Steven had a swollen lip; my ring had caught his lip and cut him. We were still a mess. I was not myself at all. This continued for weeks.

When we returned to our house, Steven's dad said to me, "You are not welcome in this family. I want you to go." "I just wanted to enjoy my son's retirement." I said, "I did too," then turned to Steven and said, "They don't understand." He hugged me. He was so sorry for all of this. The day before, Steven's paternal grandfather scolded Thomas about what he was doing and how it was besmirching the family name—the grandparents supported me.

I was utterly embarrassed. I accepted the blame and, shamefully, apologized to everyone, including Steven's boys. At this point, the story was that I had too much to drink, this was an alcohol-related incident and that I needed to completely eliminate alcohol. I agreed with everything. I was overwhelmed with shame. Jane instructed everyone to sit in a circle and hold hands so that she could lead us in prayer. Jane sat in between the boys and prayed. Then I prayed and apologized. Jane citing stress, had medicated herself with Xanax and vodka, since suffering from a headache the day before. I have no doubt that the situation was very stressful for her—still she presented as calm and in control of the ongoing situation, while I had been out of control. She had the capacity to offer support to everyone involved in these awful moments—she felt good about her role. I was broken and helpless, the symbol of all that was ugly that day. Of course, even my husband preferred what this lovely and affectionate woman, with whom he had a fond history, had to offer. For the rest of their visit I sat calmly and soberly by, watching Jane lavish Steven with constant rubbing, touching and words of support and affirmation. She was literally, physically, in the middle of my relationship with Steven—I was still alone and, in a dissociative state, my mind unable to handle all that was happening—my insides were trembling.

My parents dropped off Junior and left for home, so they weren't aware of all that had happened. My mother later told me that Steven's mother sent an email to them that was so disparaging of me they never wanted me to see it. When my mother revealed this, I told her that the incident was not alcohol-related for me at all; it was psychological, and I was still not well.

Steven's mother also relayed to Steven's paternal grandparents and other family members all that had happened. We didn't know this until Steven's paternal grandparents told us later. They defended us and shared with us the ongoing family controversy happening behind our backs. Steven's family blamed me for all that had transpired—according to them, I should never have called the police when Thomas choked Junior because that led to all the rest—to me yelling at the boys the night of the retirement party and, eventually, to Steven losing his boys.

Regrettably, in the weeks that followed, I experienced several other intensely emotional outbursts. These occurred in front of the children, but were all directed at Steven, and some of them were alcohol-related. Sometimes, Steven and I hid in our back bedroom, drinking wine and watching television just to get away from his boys, his mother and the toxic situation in which we found ourselves. It was the only way that we could feel better in those dark days. Steven's mother regularly chastised us for this behavior.

A day honoring an American war hero turned into chaos. It makes me so sad to think about everyone that attended, and especially those who traveled to honor Steven. The expected happy and joyful celebration turned into a seriously traumatic event. Of course, I feel ashamed of my part in it.

FORTY-FIVE

Manipulation of Common Sense

No children in our neighborhood were allowed to come to our house because of the accusation, excepting one child whose parents didn't know. The neighborhood women feared that Thomas would make further allegations and they all knew about Thomas's violence toward Junior on New Year's Eve. Very few children even played with Thomas outside, so he was with Steven most of the time. We had a lovely backyard and a large in-ground pool. Junior and I had looked forward to friends coming over to spend sunny Virginia Beach days at our house, enjoying the pool, as they had before Thomas and Jay's arrival. Now, the pool was empty most of the time.

It would have felt normal to talk with Jo, despite everything. Her children were in my home for months; why wouldn't we talk? I had initially hoped for polite conversation, about care of the children and ensuring that they knew love from all of us. However, Jo lost the opportunity for free dialogue and any type of verbal interaction with Steven when she leveled her first threat and she ensured this loss with the seriousness of her false allegations.

Email 7/15/2014
" *Steve,*
I will be calling Thomas and Jay tomorrow since I could not reach them tonight. Please make them available to talk to.
Thank you,
Jo"

Email 7/15/2014
"I encourage you to do so. I appreciate you not harassing me and my wife by calling my phone, threatening to call the police and sue her, repeatedly, as you did up until last week. I can produce phone records if you choose to counter what I am saying. I encourage all phone records to be brought forward to show how consistently (well beyond what has been agreed upon) you have been in contact with the boys.

I also have recently learned that you have been very active in false allegations against my wife. Those not investigated were read aloud to both of us. No authoritative person involved in any of these allegations thinks anything other than all are originating from you. No one believes that any are true and in fact discussed at length with us how to handle a jealous and angry female ex-spouse.

I am not with the boys; they are happily with their grandmother (and re-bonding after 6 months of zero contact) as I am attending an out of town important work-related event with my wife.

I have instructed the boys to respond to the daily repeated personal questions about me, my wife, my home, my stepson, that those issues not pertaining to them is not their concern and definitely not yours. They do not need to continue to be put in the middle of adult matters and should be free to enjoy their summer, friends and family. I am asking you to stop obsessing about me, my wife, my home and my stepson and to stop harassing the boys on a daily basis. They are uncomfortable because they love both of their parents and do not want to disrespect either. I am asking to allow me to have quality time with my sons without continued distractive and obsessive interference.

Thank you in advance for your cooperation and co-parenting."

Despite Steven's clear and reasonable email request, Jo did not stop calling Steven's phone. Not wanting to even hear the sound of her voice, even a message, Steven deleted them without listening or passed the phone to me.

One day in July, he passed the phone to me as she called. During less than six minutes of phone contact, Jo hung up on me three times. After the first hangup, Jo stated that "she was not going to do this," threatened to "call the police," stated that she had already "started a law suit about my blog," threatened to "start a new one," stated that I was "harassing her" (though she was the one calling repeatedly), repeatedly called me "honey" in a condescending tone and demanded that I "put Steven on the phone," and lastly, "stop touching my children." I asked her to repeat that last one. That one came from Peter.

Jo yelled. She hyperventilated the entire time, sounded angry, emotional and, most disturbingly, desperate to talk to Steven. I explained several times that she was not married to Steven anymore and that he did not want to talk to her. She was calling us, and she was free to call police or sue me. I listened to and refrained from responding with equal frenzy.

The movie adaptation of the novel *Gone Girl* by Gillian Flynn is a powerful depiction of the manipulation of common sense. There's no doubt that Ben Affleck's character, Nick, is a grade "A" ass. Women can relate to experiencing that kind of betrayal because that's what some guys do, they reuse a card that has worked in the past—Rosamund Pike's character, Amy, observes Nick taking familiar actions to pick up a younger, beautiful woman, so for a minute, we cheer for Amy. Then common-sense kicks in and, WHOA, hold on Amy.

After a dizzying amount of effort at control and manipulation, the end of the film surprises us when Amy happens upon a situation better than she planned; she comes back into her own life, she and Nick resume where they left off, and she manipulates him into staying with her. Her false "Amazing Amy" childhood comes full circle as she, a grown children's book character, desperately clutches a false life with someone that does not want her. Amy faked her own kidnapping and tried to frame her husband Nick. Nick's most insightful question, and my personal favorite, "Why do you want this?"

I was baffled by Jo's singular obsession with Steven, and then I saw *Gone Girl* and suddenly got it. Why did she want to be with Steven, knowing that he didn't want the marriage to continue? If Steven had died in battle, Jo could have created the story of a perfect marriage, family, life OR she could have painted herself a victim of Steven's abuses. Steven's legacy would've been whatever Jo wanted to create...forever.

By the time Steven was formally accused of beating Jo, the train had already left the station, and he didn't know how to defend himself. It's very difficult to anticipate the next chess move when very little is based in reality, while what is real is exaggerated.

"All of this can go away if you come back." A threat had coerced Steven into marriage, and another had worked to bring him back from separation. Why wouldn't Jo try it again? The NCIS investigation, and years later, a call to Homeland Security to shut down Steven's plans to work with the state police were the culmination of Jo's obsessive plotting, all the while relaying her stories to anyone who would listen. Finally, the false sexual abuse allegation against me. She talked and behaved as though she and Steven would unite against me. Jo spent years trying to destroy our lives, all with the hope of having Steven back and under her control. Why do you want this?

FORTY-SIX

Jo's Vengeance Manifests in Jay

"The needs of the troubled parent override the development needs of the child, with the result that the child becomes psychologically depleted and their own emotional and social progress is crippled."
~Wallerstein and Blakeslee, Second Chances

Steven, all three boys and I continued in therapy with the same therapist. Junior's blonde-haired best friend invited him on vacation with their family for several weeks. Steven and I were relieved that, completely innocent in all of this, he got a break from all of the tension and conflict in the house. Steven kept Thomas with him most of the time, and made both of his boys do chores. Jay's sexualized behaviors and comments had worsened from the previous summer. He consistently talked about anal rape and wouldn't leave other children alone, tightly hugging them, simulating masturbation and/or grabbing/rubbing them sexually. Fewer and fewer children were allowed to interact with Jay. Both boys complained constantly about not being able to play video games. Jay said, "We have people that do that work for us in Florida." Steven's mother commented that it was unfair that Junior could have a fun summer while his boys had to work. Steven responded, "They are behaving badly, mom, and need to be taught a work ethic and not get everything handed to them. That was part of the problem."

Four weeks after I had been questioned at the police station about the false sexual abuse allegation, a new-to-us social worker arrived unexpectedly at our house for the final "drop in" visit. She said that the accusation I faced was rare and the most difficult for family recovery. By this time, Thomas had admitted that the event was only a dream and that he had wanted to hurt me for putting him in jail. By the end of the investigation and this final drop-in visit, he was remorseful. The social worker went on to say that our cases were the most unique that their office had ever processed. If I had not called and flagged our cases, we would've been investigated many more times, as both Peter and Jo had called, multiple times, with other allegations. The previous allegations did not carry enough validity to warrant investigations, but they were required to investigate this sexual allegation. The social worker subtly suggested we not host Thomas and Jay in our home again, and that, in her opinion, things were only going to get worse. Per Steven's request, his mother left days after the final home visit.

Boys don't act so poorly for no reason; Steven's boys acted outwardly on behalf of Jo. Trying again to gain his family's understanding of our situation, along with their support, Steven emailed his dad, stepmother and mother. He also sent the email to his attorney who, for the first time, took Jo's aggression seriously, though he did not want to take action or notify Jo's attorney.

Email 8/3/2014

"Over the course of the boy's time here in Virginia Beach, five families confronted us about Jay's behavior. As of last week, no children in our

neighborhood were allowed to play with Jay. Jay threatened to rape children, described rape to them, dry humped several, called children sexual terms (e.g. pussy, vagina, penis, anus, fagot, had herpes, etc.). He would not stop body locking boys when they asked him to stop and could not stop touching all boys younger and one boy older.

We live in a very conservative neighborhood and these children have not been exposed to all of this. We have lost all of our friends as well. Our home is exactly opposite of how it is when it is Sabrina, Junior and me.

Sabrina left with Junior to try and salvage a summer for him. She is with her brothers in Myrtle Beach. On the trip there, Junior relayed serious acts of sexual abuse from Jay.

- Jay threatened to rape Junior 20-30 times a day
- Jay described how he was going to rape Junior (take his clothes off, beat him, stick his penis in his anus)
- Jay talked about male on male sex constantly to Junior
- Jay locked Junior in a closet and tried to pull his pants down and rape him
- Junior has woken up to Jay dry humping the covers next to him (last summer it started)
- Jay threatened to stick his fingers in Junior's anus
- Jay threatened to rape Junior with a knife
- In the middle of one day, with the door open, Jay stroked his penis, made it hard and told Junior he was going to rape him with it. Junior ran out of the room
- Jay kicked Junior so hard in the butt his sneaker went up Junior's butt about half an inch
- Jay kicked Junior directly in the penis so hard I had to take him out of church days later to check on him he was in so much pain
- Jay head butted Junior in the penis so hard it hurt for quite a long time
- Jay took a butcher knife from the kitchen, scraped the hair off of his arm, then simulated slitting his wrists, by dragging the knife over his skin, and told Junior he was going to kill himself, several times
- Junior feared telling us because he believed Jay would rape and kill him

Not knowing what to do, we contacted the social worker involved with allegations of sexual abuse against Sabrina. She said this was a severe case *and reported it to the sex crimes unit as a follow up to her investigation. During her interview Sabrina stated that she believed the boys were being sexually assaulted, just not by her. They need to interview Junior for the case to move forward. I want all this documented anticipating it will be twisted and distorted making it our fault somehow. Jay returned to FL 10 days early, today. Thanks.*

V/R,

Steve"

After Junior's forensic interview, the detectives called me into a room, by myself. They confronted me about Steven's future visitation with his boys. They all agreed that he should cut ties with both of them and, if not, I should think about leaving him. They said that they see a lot of step-sibling issues, but they're primarily sexual exploration. They said that they had rarely seen this level of violence before and that Jay was grooming Junior to act out his threats, and soon. Jay was not charged because Junior did not disclose an injury. If Junior had mentioned the kicks Jay inflicted, he would've been charged and had a hearing, as Thomas had. Junior believing that Jay's kicks were accidents, as Jay had told him, did not think that he should mention them in the interview. It was good that I finally took Junior away to Myrtle Beach. Still, I felt tremendous guilt for not having left immediately after Thomas's allegations.

Junior first relayed to me all of Jay's abuses just a few miles into our drive to Myrtle Beach. He hugged my arm tightly and cried while he told me. He also told me that the previous summer, both Thomas and Jay wrapped him in blankets when he called Steven "Dad," laying on him so that he couldn't breathe. While the older boys had been threatening, and had begun to act violently privately, this summer Jay threatened Junior while in the same room as Steven and me, saying, "See I can do what I want to you right in front of them and they won't do anything." I asked Junior why he hadn't told me, and he said that I always told him he was my number one, so he thought Steven's boys were his number ones and that we would take their side. To watch Junior, again in anguish, knowing that I had been there and didn't protect him, added to the deterioration of my mental state, added to my guilt and made me question my decisions about Steven. While I had no option to escape my situation, I could walk away with Junior so that neither of us would have to endure anymore abuses toward him.

Thomas returned to Florida, leaving only Jay and Steven in the house. Thomas mentioned before he left that he had several friends whose parents had also divorced and that none of their situations were anything like his. Steven tried to help Jay understand that his behaviors were wrong and that his loss of friendships was a natural consequence. Jay laid around, playing video games, showing no remorse or understanding of the situation. Steven had no training in how to deal with these traumatic situations and wanted me and Junior to come back home. He sent Jay home to Florida early, and Junior and I returned home to get ready to move back to Kentucky.

Steven had given a new iPhone to Thomas for his birthday and told him that if the boy turned it off, he would not fight for visitation again. It took too much of a toll on everyone, it was too expensive and completely unnecessary. Thomas said that he understood and texted Steven during his trip back, informing his dad about his flights and what he was doing. When the plane touched down in Florida the phone was turned off and never turned on again.

When Jo sent an email, copying her attorney and Steven's stating what needed to be worked out before the next visitation, Steven responded that it wouldn't be necessary—he did (and still does) not wish to continue visitations with his boys.

FORTY-SEVEN

All the While Peter Continues

Email 7/18/2014

"Ms. Brown:

Based on the groundswell of support steadily flowing in, both nationally and internationally, I imagine you have learned of the tragic loss of Jack's [Peter's older brother] daughter, my niece (age 6, though media is reporting 7). Despite everything, I recognize you knew and appreciated her as her aunt, and recall interacting with her in Toronto and her staying in our home in Lexington. Your daughters are of course devastated.

I attach a link to today's National Post and Toronto Star stories, below (there are many others to peruse as well).

The visitation is in Toronto on Sunday and the funeral is on Monday. I would like Junior picked up tomorrow (Saturday) morning in order to have him here for Sunday's events. I won't get into any proposed details until I hear back from you. Please respond as soon as possible. I would certainly appreciate it if you were willing to drive part of the way to meet.

Thank-you,
Peter"

Email 7/18/2014 (from me):

I am very sorry for you and your family's loss. It is tragic. A child's sudden death affects everyone.

Unfortunately, at this time, we are still left with only trying to understand bizarre emails and questionable motives surrounding a court ordered visitation I had initiated and encouraged. The last meaningful conversation you both had being talking excitedly about his trip to Canada; a countdown months leading up to the visit and devastation in the days following your unexplainable disappearance; not returning Junior's many emotional phone calls, messages and text messages to you and his sisters. Junior grieved your death for those three days.

Despite these very sad events, Steve and my concerns remain the same. Junior cannot, under any circumstance, cross an international border. You are free to visit Junior at any time here in Virginia Beach with a third party, until we understand what has happened and why you have abandoned him, instead of building back your relationship. Steve and I remain committed to assisting in repairing your relationship to Junior; he loving both parents. We actually talked about how to re-introduce you into his life today, with our family therapist. We decided it would be best for you to tell him about his cousin, on speaker phone, with our therapist. She is willing to talk to you prior to this call (her fee is $70/hour). We believe this is the best and healthiest starting point. We have a long way to go for trust to be established, for anything more. For Junior to enter into one of the most emotionally charged events for human beings, being estranged from his father and sisters for over half a year could be traumatic for him. If you and the girls had been making an effort to maintain a bond with Junior, taking any opportunity available to visit and communicate, in a manner promoting love and respect for both parents, we would be working out flight plans.

When things settle down, please let me know when you would like to arrange a phone conversation with Junior, to tell him about his cousin, and I will arrange everything. We have established appointments that we could use for this purpose. Again, you can speak with her prior to the call if you would like.

Condolences to you, your family and especially [the mother].

Email 8/11/2014

"*It was unconscionable you determined to block Junior from being with his* family following the tragic, sudden death of your niece, his cousin, but most unfortunately it was predictable. Junior's cousin who you recall grew up in the shadow of his older brother's death, asked me about Junior in the days leading up to his sister's funeral. I had to tell him you were blocking him from coming. He shook his head and said, "I figured she wouldn't let him come." That's essentially what everyone I interacted with said. More people than you would likely imagine were greatly disappointed at Junior's absence, the result of your unilateral, harmful decision.

Your suggestion I pay a therapist in order to have a phone interaction with my son was again a unilateral decision without concern for Junior. I don't require a therapist to interact with a bereaved child, especially my own. You have the luxury of a fellow co-parent who is a dedicated parent of more than two decades, a trained therapist, and someone with experience specifically in bereavement therapy for children and youth, and yet you somehow reached the conclusion Junior shouldn't attend his cousin's funeral with me present.

I am ready to care for Junior at any point going forward. His sisters, grandparents, and extended family are all waiting to embrace Junior who has been so maliciously alienated from his family. Will you consider ending the punishment you are inflicting on Junior. What could he have done to deserve this treatment?"

Email 9/16/2014

"Ms. Brown,

I was hoping to have received a reply regarding the concerns I expressed in an August email. I still don't have a physical address for Junior. The reason I contacted the Virginia Beach Police was simply to locate Junior, and ensure his safety. Please let me know what you have planned for Junior. Where is he living? Where is he attending or to attend school? Will you consider beginning to allow Junior regular contact with me?

I sent another child support cheque to the Virginia Beach residence by certified mail last month. The tracking of the package indicated that after it was delivered and no one initially received it, it sat at your post office for one week before it was returned to me in Ottawa. I am ready to again pay the $30 to have another package delivered securely through certified mail, but I require an address.

I plan to be in Lexington over the first weekend in October. This summer you raised concern over Junior traveling with me to my home in Ottawa and to attend his cousin's funeral in Toronto. I'm not sure I understand that entirely, but in the meantime I would like to have a low key, highly predictable weekend with Junior in Lexington.

...I am very anxious to spend time with Junior. I would like to put together a fantastic weekend. I think it also vitally important that I have opportunity to speak to Junior about the death of his cousin, and provide him opportunity to begin to grieve this profound loss. If he already knows about the death, I would like to meet him where he is in his process. There are so many evidences of light permeating the darkness of this tragedy.

...Thank-you for your consideration, and I look forward to your reply.

Peter"

Email 9/16/2014 (from me):

As I have said, your first interaction with Junior needs to be with a therapist present. He needs to build back trust with you following your bizarre disappearance over spring break. He was devastated for days thinking you were dead. Let me know if you are willing to participate. What happened over spring break does not seem mentally stable and was emotionally abusive to Junior....

Email 11/23/2014

"Ms. Brown:

I'm writing two days before our son Junior's eleventh birthday. I am again reminding you of your unconscionable decision to alienate him from me, his father, and his sisters. Junior is also alienated from his grandparents and a host of other extended family. I don't know what possible construal in your mind finds Junior better off as a result of your attempt to cut him off from almost all of his immediate family, those he loves dearly, those closest to him. What a crushing burden Junior has – needlessly – been made to endure.

I know first hand, having provided professional therapy and therapeutic services to dozens of severely troubled children and youth on the losing end of a parent's misguided decision, the tremendous emotional impact of this kind of short-sightedness. It's never worth it.

Clearly this won't stand, as we were awarded joint custody of Junior. On the other end of this most recent period of alienation what is to happen? How *have you reached the conclusion you were left ongoing to make unilateral decisions regarding Junior's future? I assure you, but you know this, Junior will be in a much better place when he resumes a life with all of his family, not his mother exclusively and as a result of coercion.*

I would like to ask you again, as I've done many times before, to take the adult perspective and place Junior's needs at the forefront. I ask you to begin facilitating a visitation plan for Junior within the next couple of days. Junior will be beyond thrilled to spend Christmas in Ottawa with family he has missed for so long now. Imagine what it would mean to Junior to be reunited with his sisters after an entire year of alienation; they have so much to relay to him. What better Christmas gift could you possible give him?

….Thank-you for your understanding. I trust you will consider afresh the newness that comes with the beginning of the liturgical year, falling next Sunday. Advent provides opportunity for repentance and the anticipation of something entirely unexpected.

Peter"

FORTY-EIGHT

When Fragile, Handle with Care

Hands down, 2013 and 2014 were some of the worst and the best of times for both Steven and me. The summer of 2014 was the worst in either of our lives. Shortly after Junior and I returned to Virginia Beach, one of my favorite aunts died and we decided to get out of town and attend her memorial service at my cousin's house. We decided to stay with my cousin as she had space and had been a support through everything with Peter. I looked forward to the love and encouragement that she and her husband were sure to give us. About an hour after we arrived, as Steven I relayed all that had happened during the past months, she became very aggressive with me, assuming that she was defending Steven, and she was escalating. She said, "Those are his kids and you can't do what you did; you need to support them, those are his kids." She spoke from her own story, in which she viewed herself as sacrificing a great deal in support of her stepchildren. She had been drinking so she probably wasn't hearing me and my pain. I broke again, pushed her away and screamed for her to stop. She is very tough and came right back at me, and we had a literal knock-down, drag-out through the house. In the end, she made me sleep in my car and Steven came out with me. This time, unfortunately Junior witnessed everything.

The next day was the memorial service and my parents attended. When my mother asked where I was, my cousin reported that I was jealous of her and Steven, and that she made me sleep in my car. Steven was very supportive and so were my parents. They were concerned for my well-being, knowing the full story.

After the service, I approached my cousin at the urging of her daughter. She quickly responded that "Nothing is my fault," and that my "stories" are not believable. I responded in disbelief because she had been at my house in Kentucky when Peter finally left and she saw the beginning of my daughter's alienation from me firsthand. I told her that I was, at times, a horrible person and that I take responsibility for what I have done. I was triggered. It was not pretty. I was not pretty. I also said that I could not have made up what happened during the past summer. It was simply a nightmare. She would not relent; she and I have not spoken since.

This particular event is important because it shows the damage that PAS inflicts—not only on the child-(ren) but also on the alienated parent. Domestic violence, personality disorders and PAS are so intermingled. I hope that our story helps in understanding how to identify the perpetrator-alienator, the deep psychological effects and consequences of PAS. This understanding can help victims and their children sooner.

FORTY-NINE

A New Judge, A New Audience for Peter

We moved to the camp in Kentucky shortly after we returned to Virginia Beach from the memorial service. Weeks later, state police arrived at our home as we sat around a campfire with all the pets, laughing. We thought they were there because Steven is going to build a shooting range and had already talked with Kentucky State Police about using it for training. The trooper apologetically told us the nature of his visit. Peter had made a false allegation and used almost exactly Jo's language about Steven being armed and dangerous.

Any time that Steven or I see anything that looks court-related, we get anxious. As Peter was still making false allegations, I panicked when I received a motion in the mail. Peter wanted to move our case to the county where Steven, Junior and I had moved, a different county than the one where our case had been all along. By this time, I knew what he was doing—we had seen it with Jo, and I had been warned about this from experts: Peter sought a fresh audience because the judge in our case had called him out on both domestic violence and PAS. He represented himself and didn't incur the same expenses that I faced. He wanted to create chaos again, knowing that it would likely take a while for me to once more prove his abuse. I got in touch with my attorney, Robin. She responded that the case had been so long and hostile that it needed to stay within the court that knew the history. She won this argument, but our judge had retired, so we had a new judge.

Six months later I received another motion to appear in court in front of the new judge. Peter wanted to reinstate timeshare with Junior and was suing me over my blog.

The judge thought that Peter was an attorney representing himself due to his suit and his still charming first impression. When he introduced himself, she smiled and asked him about his motion. She told him that things were going to change, and that she would make sure that he saw his son regularly. She then turned to me and asked why I had prevented Peter from seeing or communicating with his son for so long. Robin jumped up and said, "Your Honor, I don't think you have read my response." The judge then read the email exchanges about spring break, concern over Junior's international travel and my request that a therapist facilitate Peter's next communication with Junior. As she read you could visibly see the anger pass over her face. Steven and I will never forget her face when she looked up. She glared at Peter and asked him if he was at the exchange location in Virginia Beach or not. He talked in circles much like the text of an email that he sent to me a month later (below, 6/10/2015). He finally admitted he had not made the trip and then quickly turned the blame to me. The judge interrupted and said that we needed to schedule another private hearing, as this was too much to deal with during the family court hearing hour. She said that if she allowed visitation the first thing out of Peter's mouth would be to place all blame on me—she would need to get to the bottom of the spring break incident before he could have any visitation. She did not even allow supervised visitation. She then turned to me and recommended that we use Skype for communication, and not the phone, so if Peter talked about spring break or disparaged me, I could shut it down.

About my blog, she recommended he stop sending me emails.

Email 6/10/2015

"Ms. Brown:

I am writing again to ask you to facilitate, or have someone else facilitate, regular phone contact between Junior and I. It has now been one month since our judge gave clear instruction I was to begin phone contact with Junior. Additionally, Junior's grandparents, John and Elaine Walton, would like to speak to Junior, either by phone or Skype. Please let me know what times during the week Junior is available.

As you well know, the references to spring break 2014 aren't relevant. I was never sent the final signed order to come from the court, which did NOT include time-sharing over Junior's spring break. You knew this but I did not, never having received the final signed order (I didn't confirm the exclusion of spring break 2014 until I went to the courthouse to dig the order out of the file while I was in Lexington, October 2013. At that time, you may recall refusing to allow me to spend any time with Junior).

[Email 7/29/2013, from Peter, "The Judge [the first judge in our case] ordered a time-sharing agreement going forward, allowing me time with Junior in August, Thanksgiving, the two days in Myrtle Beach December 23rd and 24th, and his spring break from school, 2014."]

I was in Virginia Beach to pick up my son, but he wasn't at the agreed upon location. The dramatic suitcase in hand-sitting on the curb-waiting scene, as described in court, didn't occur. Your truck was not there when you said it was, only a police cruiser and a few cars not belonging to you, off to the side. No Junior. After driving all that way, I waited and waited in the lot, and continued to watch the parking lot where we'd done an exchange a few months before, but Junior never arrived.

You apparently were repeating the same stunt you attempted over Junior's spring break 2013 when you filed an EPO against me. And the judge's admonition to you in August 2013, when you dismissed the groundless EPO, wouldn't apply in Virginia. Even in this very email chain you threaten to file a motion against me for harassment - because I'm inquiring about phone times.

All I wanted was to spend time with my son, and that's all he wanted as well. For his sake I didn't agree to a Skype session with a therapist, in order to explain how I was prevented from seeing him over his spring break.

It's so unfortunate the court needs to become involved at all, but clearly it's necessary for Junior's sake. Please comply with the judge's instruction concerning phone contact. Additionally, please consider Junior's grandparents would like to speak with him from time to time. They, like me, miss Junior every day.

Thank-you,
Peter"

During Easter weekend in 2013 (which was not his year to have timeshare for this vacation), Peter sent threatening emails to me about eventually taking my son, as he had already taken my girls. He owed thousands of dollars in child support. I feared he would kidnap my son and I could envision Peter pontificating as he did so often, "What would be in his best interest would be to stay here with me." What was different this time is that I knew that I didn't have to accept the fear; I filed an EPO. The policy in our county's family court was "one family, one judge," so I was seen before the judge in our divorce case. He knew the background, agreed with my concerns and granted me the EPO. The Walton's eluded the service of the order. Peter was out of the country. Still, his brother Ben could be served and be asked to communicate the notice.

On several occasions, Ben was not at home to accept service. Our hearing was in August 2013. I agreed to drop the EPO in favor of an order that Peter not be allowed to have any verbal communication with me again; only email. And email communication would need to be only about logistics concerning Junior, he was not to disparage me or talk about the past.

The initial email: 3/26/2013

"Sabrina,

I want to let you know that I have been able to work out travel to Lexington over the Easter weekend. This, of course, is great news for me and great news for Junior. I hope you are able to allow yourself to recognize this reality as well, for the good of Junio...We will plan on arriving in Lexington in three days, on Friday (March 29), in time to pick up Junior from Elementary school at the end of the school day. I will plan on contacting the school tomorrow to let them know about the arrangement. Please make sure to send a note to indicate that I will arrive before the end of the school day, and that you fully recognize that Junior will leave with me....Please confirm that you understand the arrangement for this weekend

Thank-you and please remember to send a note with Junior to school,
Peter"

Email 5/10/2015

"Ms. Brown:

I called earlier today and got no answer. I'll call your number until you help me determine the best number for Junior.

Thank-you,
Peter"

Email 5/18/2015 (from me):

Junior will be available by Skype and with a counselor present to monitor the conversation. Since you and my daughter found it so amusing last Skype when questioned about your disappearance over last spring break, it is in Junior's best interest to have a therapist present.

Blowing up my phone on mothers' day and randomly is not appropriate given the history of domestic violence. If it continues, I will be forced to file another motion to stop this harassment.

Email 5/19/2015

"Ms. Brown:

I've begun calling your number intermittently, only after our appearance in Family Court on May 8th. I called a few times over the weekend of May 8th thru 10th because I was excited to finally have opportunity to speak to

Junior after nearly a year, and I knew he would welcome the chance to finally speak to me. You didn't permit a call over the entire weekend and you haven't since. I last called this past Friday, twice. There was no answer and no return call.

The Judge made clear on the 8th that phone contact between Junior and I should begin. The Judge said nothing about resuming contact with Junior via Skype nor the involvement of a therapist. I was crushed that I had travelled to Lexington at great expense and wasn't able to spend any time with my son over the entire weekend, after not seeing him since December 2013. The only consolation from my standpoint was being permitted phone contact, but I should have known this too would become one more fiasco.

I can assure you I find nothing amusing about being alienated from by son. File your motion if you wish. I'm simply following the Judge's crystal clear permission for phone contact to begin. The reason I emphasized with the Judge that I need to see the written order from your attorney before it's submitted to the court is to ensure there are no omissions, like the omitted permission for me to spend time with Junior over the course of his 2014 spring break, which was granted by the former Judge but omitted from the final order written by your attorney.

Peter"

Email 5/21/2015

"Ms. Brown:

As indicated, I attempted to reach Junior by phone last evening at 7pm. I called one time. There was no answer and no return call. The Judge was unambiguous in stating that phone contact between Junior and I should begin. How do you think this can best be accomplished?

Thank-you,

Peter"

Email 6/9/2015

"Ms. Brown:

I am writing again to ask you to facilitate, or have someone else facilitate, regular phone contact between Junior and I. It has now been one month since the Judge gave clear instruction I was to begin phone contact with Junior. Additionally, Junior's grandparents, would like to speak to Junior, either by *phone or Skype. Please let me know what times during the week Junior is available.*

As you well know, the references to spring break 2014 aren't relevant. I was never sent the final signed order to come from the court, which did NOT include time-sharing over Junior's spring break. You knew this but I did not, never having received the final signed order (I didn't confirm the exclusion of spring break 2014 until I went to the courthouse to dig the order out of the file while I was in Lexington, October 2014. At that time you may recall refusing to allow me to spend any time with Junior).

I was in Virginia Beach to pick up my son, but he wasn't at the agreed upon location. The dramatic suitcase in hand-sitting on the curb-waiting scene, as described in court, didn't occur. Your truck was not there when you said it was, only a police cruiser and a few cars not belonging to you, off to the side. No Junior. After driving all that way, I waited and waited in the lot, and continued to watch the parking lot where we'd done an exchange a few months before, but Junior never arrived.

You apparently were repeating the same stunt you attempted over Junior's spring break 2013 when you filed an EPO against me. The Judge's admonition to you in August 2013, when you dismissed the groundless EPO, wouldn't apply in Virginia. Even in this very email chain you threaten to file a motion against me for harassment - because I'm inquiring about phone times.

All I wanted was to spend time with my son, and that's all he wanted as well. For his sake I didn't agree to a Skype session with a therapist, in order to explain how I was prevented from seeing him over his spring break.

It's so unfortunate the court needs to become involved at all, but clearly it's necessary for Junior's sake. Please comply with the Judge's instruction concerning phone contact. Additionally, please consider Junior's grandparents would like to speak with him from time to time. They, like me, miss Junior every day.

Thank-you,
Peter"

Email 7/8/2015

"Ms. Brown:

I am writing concerning your refusal to facilitate phone contact as the Judge made clear was to begin following the hearing in Family Court, May

8th. Today marks two months. What has Junior done to, in your mind, deserve this ongoing punishment? Or, is Junior not part of your consideration at all?

I'm simply asking that you comply with the Judge's clear instruction. Additionally, last month, I asked in an email that you allow for Junior's grandparents to have opportunity to speak with their grandson over the phone or through a Skype session, and this has not happened.

Please let me know as soon as possible when Junior is available to speak to me by phone - anytime today can work; anytime tomorrow can work. As the Judge said on May 8th, "this shouldn't be difficult," in reference to the matter of working out an agreeable arrangement for Junior to benefit from spending time with both his parents. I quite agree. Why is it so difficult to merely facilitate phone calls when conducive to your schedule?

For Junior's sake, I thank you for your immediate attention.
Peter"

Email 8/8/2015

"Ms. Brown:

Yet another month has passed by without reply to my emails regarding the Judge's clear directive of May 8, 2015 that phone contact should begin between Junior and me, in anticipation of the next family court hearing. I've additionally asked that you facilitate phone or Skype contact between Junior and his grandparents.

I am asking - as I've asked similarly many times before, over the course of years now - that you change course, for Junior's sake, and in this case begin to comply with the Judge's clear directive. Please - please - begin to consider Junior and the traumatic impact parental alienation is having on his development.

What time today (Sunday) can Junior and I have a conversation by phone?

Thank-you for your immediate consideration.
Peter Walton"

FIFTY

A Sociopath Will Not Concede, No Matter the Cost

Peter had scheduled the hearing with the judge back in May and now he failed to appear. The judge asked if I had Peter's phone number and I provided it. There was no answer, so I gave her every number that I had for him and she finally got through.

The judge again questioned him about the spring break episode. At the first hearing he admitted to not being at the drop off, but now he claimed that he was there. He even challenged my attorney to check the border crossing records to prove that he had, indeed, crossed the border to pick up Junior and that I had, with my "usual histrionics" prevented him from seeing Junior. He claimed that he drove a day to pick up Junior, waited, and then drove all the way back to Canada.

The judge stayed resolutely on topic, bringing the conversation back to spring break more than a dozen times. She finally stated that she was concerned about Peter's mental health.

Peter was challenged by a beautiful, powerful and intelligent woman.

Peter's anger was so intense you could hear his words coming out through clenched teeth. He, without hesitation, flipped back "But I'm not the one with the mental illness, *she* is the one with mental illnesses...*she*...is a *borderline.*" The judge responded that she did not see any sign of mental illness in me but was so concerned about him that she ordered a full psychological evaluation to be done in Lexington. She also ordered therapy for him with a court-appointed therapist.

She ordered that Peter's therapy continue until he explained himself and took responsibility for the severe psychological abuse that he had inflicted on his son. Only after the therapist was satisfied that Peter was remorseful, and that Junior was safe from any further abuse, would there be a re-introduction period between Junior and Peter, always with the court-ordered therapist present. Until all orders were met, Peter could not have ANY communication with Junior.

Finally, on August 31, 2015, five year after I had taken my first stand against Peter, he could no longer contact me or Junior—Junior, was six at the beginning of this journey, was turning twelve just a few months after its conclusion.

A short time later, Peter sent a letter to the judge explaining that he did not have the money for even the initial psychological evaluation. He had the money when he was fighting for sole custody; when the focus was on me, he came up with his monetary portion of court-ordered therapy for the two minor children during our custody litigation. That court-ordered therapy time was used to "help" my middle daughter deal with my "borderline personality disorder," as directed by Peter. This therapy time was also used to hurl continued allegations at me, and I spent most of my time defending myself. Now that he was unable to manipulate the system, he did not have the money to participate.

Additionally, the judge's orders were similar to what Steven and I thought would be the best way for Peter to resume contact with Junior, and without the extra cost and inconvenience of travel and time off of work.

A year later, Peter had not taken any action toward fulfilling the orders of the court. And he probably never would.

Relief at last.

FIFTY-ONE

Relief?

In 2016, Steven and I began the process of terminating Peter's parental rights along with Junior's adoption by Steven. Stepfather and stepson both very much wanted this official adoption. During this time, Junior began using his phone more that I felt was appropriate for his age, so I checked it one evening. I accidentally came across some disturbing messages.

Junior opened a social networking account in order to talk to some of his school and baseball friends.

My middle daughter along with a cousin on Peter's side of the family had together, targeted Junior. They bullied him, blamed him and were cruel and hateful. They made comments like, "you traitor."

When I asked him about it the next morning, he said that he became very depressed about it, but he hadn't told me because he wanted to protect me.

Around that same time, I started to receive random phone calls from both of my daughters demanding that I put Junior on the phone right then. It is interesting that during the same time that Peter was not fulfilling the orders of the court, Peter was not allowed to communicate with me or Junior and could no longer manipulate us or the court, my daughters suddenly decided to communicate with their brother, perhaps independently, perhaps not.

Junior's big sisters do not understand how their brother has grieved their living death and to pass the phone would invalidate his years of grief. Their little brother needs more than a flippant phone conversation, one that would only make them feel better while leaving him feeling abandoned once again.

I talked to Junior about their phone calls and their communications by mail. I told him that I needed to protect him from their unpredictability and from further abuse. They had not yet given a reason for not taking his calls during those traumatic three days of the spring break episode and they had not apologized. I explained that he did not yet have the capabilities to process the emotional weight with which they would try to burden him. I knew, because I had heard it over Skype, that the first thing that they would say would be something like: "We miss you, we hope you can come visit us in Canada soon, so many people miss you." These statements seem innocent, but they are highly charged with emotion. With these statements they put the burden on Junior to help them feel better. They make him feel responsible for helping them to not miss him. If he doesn't come to see them, from this perspective, he is responsible for their pain. How could he possibly change court orders and dictate visitation with them and/or Peter? No, I can't allow this, as it would put him in a position, once again, to feel shame without knowing what to do and all of it being out of his control.

Instead of being upset by what I said, Junior relayed to me that his sisters had begged—six at the time—to move with them to Peter's apartment when they initially moved out of my home. At that time, he told them he wanted to stay with me. I am amazed that Junior was not alienated from me, considering the amount of pressure that people very important to his life put on him and him being the youngest (typically easiest to influence) of all Steven's and my children.

He Married a Sociopath

These are the last correspondences to Junior from Peter, which followed the May hearing, with the new judge:

A card:
Hi Junior! Happy Easter (As Catholics we remain in the Easter season until Ascension Sunday on May 8th. That's when Jesus left the ground and went to live with the Father in heaven). I miss you every day, Junior. I can't wait until we are together again. We have a lot to catch up on and [your sisters] miss you too, and so do a lot of others, like your grandparents. I love you Junior and I'm proud of you! Dad--Feel free to call me anytime (phone and email)."

At Christmas that year Peter sent a crucifix and a Saint card to Junior.

In July of 2017 Steven entered a Petition For Adoption in Family Court and I hired a Warning Order Attorney to notify Peter. It included an order terminating Peter Walton's parental rights and a judgment of Adoption entered where the 'infant' is adopted by the Petitioner as his heir at law and that Petitioner be awarded full parental care, custody, and control of infant child; and that his name be changed to *Steven Brown, Junior*.

After fifty days we could proceed with the adoption. We did not hear anything from Peter during the fifty days; he could've challenged the Petition For Adoption.

A card from John Walton (Peter's father):
"Dear Junior, Your grandmom and I think of you every day. We are too lonely for you and we hope and pray you are okay. [Sisters] are doing well-- working hard in Ottawa. Your dad keeps hoping we will all be able to get together soon. I think you are going to have a birthday soon. I'd love to be in the room when you blow out the candles. I remember our visit in Ottawa, looking

over the Ottawa river. I've got your bike hanging on the wall in our garage and your toys are kept safe downstairs. We love you more than we can say on paper. Please be safe and let's hope we can be together soon. When I pray for you I pray for your mom, dad [sisters].

Another card from Peter's parents asked Junior to set up a sit down with everyone, including his sisters and Steven.

And the last communication:

Email 9/29/2017

"Dear Sabrina,

I hope that you, Steve and Junior are enjoying this season. Elaine and I are coming to Kentucky for Canadian Thanksgiving, October 5 to 8. We are lonely for Junior and wondered if you would allow us to take him for lunch or some other brief visit. We would conform to any expectation you might place on the visit, including your joining us. We long to see him and would hope to affirm him in every way. Elaine joins me in wishing you God's very best.

Sincerely,

John (and Elaine)"

Steven had a dream the other night where he answered my phone and it was my oldest daughter. She named herself and he said, "It can't be you, you're dead." He has witnessed my grief over my daughters and perhaps unconsciously equates it to the grief he experiences over his dead "brothers." Junior has also witnessed this grief as he, himself, has grieved. He has been diagnosed with PTSD from child abandonment and from the abuse he suffered from Steven's children. For Peter's parents to now contact me so casually is triggering and traumatizing. Steven is raising Junior with me, so he gets to weigh in on Junior's communication with his sisters. He thinks that a casual, yet forceful re-entrance into Junior's life would affect him as it does me—by triggering and traumatizing him. Peter's family need to slowly earn back Junior's trust if they are to ease back into his life.

My oldest daughter sent emails on 8/20/2017 and 8/25/2017, just shy of the August 28, 2017 end of the fifty-day waiting period after which Steven would be able to proceed with Junior's adoption. I didn't want to do anything to interfere with the adoption and my oldest, in her emails and phone calls to me, started making false accusations about me and blaming me completely for her alienation from Junior, so I did not reply until after the fifty-day period.

Dear Daughter,

I appreciate your love and concern for Junior. Steve and I are always open to healing and restoration. A sudden communication would be traumatic for Junior and honestly, I don't think he would be open to it at this point. If you are willing, could we first establish boundaries for his protection? And perhaps an ongoing schedule of communication so loved ones don't come and go into and out of his life? Please let me know if you are interested. Love, Mother

Daughter,

I am not blowing you off, it just so happens that we have a lot going on right now, especially Junior, and this is a very big deal. We have some events coming up at our camp in the next few weeks and when we get through them, we will be able to better respond. Love, Mother

FIFTY-TWO

Regret

Unfortunately, life involves regret. Our regret has to do with our desires for our children. If we had met earlier, we would have wanted a large family. Meeting later in life, we knew that blending our five children would be challenging, but we both fully embraced being stepparents. Over the years we have traveled a lot and have talked about how much different activities would appeal to each of our unique children.

We have an enormous love for each other—or it would not have survived what we battled. Stir in biology and chemistry that is out of this world, and the desire to procreate becomes overwhelming. Steven is a fantastic father to Junior. He is a role model just as he has been to many other young men during his career. Children seem to be drawn to him. Our lovely, special needs niece pushes me aside to get to Uncle Steve and climbs up on his lap, wanting for him to rub her head. All of my (now our) nieces and nephews love their Uncle Steve. His message from God to start a camp for middle school boys from fatherless homes did not come out of nowhere. Steven is a good man.

Steven's strong desire to have children with me, came before my desire. I never dreamed of starting over; I envisioned travel, and exciting trips and more and more freedom to pursue my goals as Junior became more independent. I've been caring for children since age nineteen. Nonetheless my desire came, and we decided to proceed with In Vitro Fertilization (IVF). We were so excited to have a baby and add to our family. We went through three rounds of IVF, starting shortly after we moved back to Kentucky in 2014. In the first round, one almost made it to implantation. In the second round, two embryos almost made it. In the third round, none of the eggs fertilized. IVF is a complicated, exhausting and expensive process. I was emotional, tired, gaining a lot of weight and dealing with a myriad of blood work and shots. The worst part, of course, was waiting and hoping for good news, then facing the bad news. We knew it was a long shot; this didn't make it any less painful.

FIFTY-THREE

Our Next Chapter

When we're in the midst of them, it's hard to understand why we go through terrible things and they seem unsurmountable at times—impossible to endure. My road has been difficult, and life has not been fair, I can't forget falling into what felt like a black hole, with no hope of ever getting out. Never in my wildest dreams did I think that, when I gave birth and devoted decades to children, that these children of mine would be taken from me. I never dreamed that my little six-year-old would be so close to being taken into foster care. Reflecting on this road, I sometimes wish that I could go back and drive another way, make different choices.

When I lived with Peter there was no Yoga for me, there were no unhurried talks with anyone, no manicures or pedicures, no salon haircuts. There was constant multi-tasking, guilty feelings when I wasn't either earning money or with my children. Even in the months I was a "stay-at-home-mom," I worked part time to make ends meet. I was always rushing, rushing to get home, to pick children up from school, take them to ballet, voice lessons and doctor's appointments. My life was taking care of everyone else, I couldn't even do my job in peace. I rushed to accomplish my job responsibilities. I rushed to the restroom. I was often in a sweat.

I never considered that I needed to take care of myself in order to be a better person and mother. Of course, I was a high-strung person; of course, I seemed crazy. In spite of this, I always maintained employment, and always sought desperately to increase my pay. Knowing that I would be the only parent responsible for the finances, nearly always working two or three jobs, I went into a field where the job opportunities were the best, not necessarily the one that I wanted, went to school for a total of twenty-five years and raised three children (the second to age sixteen).

Now, I see more clearly. I believe in free will and in evil; I know that bad things are going to happen to all of us. I also believe in redemption. If we can bear getting out of bed during those horrible times, and look up with belief and patience, we can see God's beauty and good intentions everywhere. My best days are when I'm not rushing, when I can pause and revel in the warmth of all the blessings and love surrounding me. I have again found my organic, positive, energetic self—most days.

One afternoon, during Junior's baseball season, I was running late at work and called Steven. He said, "Why don't you stop at the gym and take your time, I can take care of Junior." It was a comforting feeling to take my time and come home to warm greetings, knowing that Junior was well cared for, exactly where and with whom he wanted to be. Steven got Junior ready for baseball, had him lie down before practice and made sure that he had a snack and a water bottle for practice. When I got home, they were building a fire, laughing and playing with our many pets and having snacks while waiting for me for dinner. This may seem simple, but having a parenting partner is new for me, and taking my time is a great luxury.

After the 2015 holidays, Steven went on a Wounded Warrior trip.

One night while he was away, Junior and I went out for dinner, just the two of us. I asked Junior how the holidays were and how he felt about not having Peter or his sisters in his life. He said, "They don't make me feel good, so I don't think about them. When I do, I change my thinking." He then looked at me as if to say, "Mom, we can talk about this if YOU need to, but I'd rather talk about today." He then proceeded to talk about his school, his teachers and his science fair project. Junior learned this hard life lesson and powerful skill at age twelve: to train one's own mind to deal with enormous grief. He's also learned to work through difficulties, solve problems and not be intimidated if he doesn't succeed at first. I watch him do odd jobs around the house (e.g., hanging curtain rods), get frustrated, overcome the frustration, solve the problem and finish. It's remarkable to observe his development under Steven's fathering.

On January 18, 2018 Steven adopted Junior and his name, on his birth certificate, changed to Steven Brown, Jr.; the two of them made this decision, together. Everyone in the courtroom, knowing some of my story, was elated, it was an emotional moment. The three of us were overjoyed, our overall thoughts and feelings were of closure and great comfort.

On the way home Steven and Junior bickered like father and teenage son. I don't think either had felt it was completely safe to behave so normally before this most important event.

Looking back at my first years together with Steven, we've had to work at it...hard. We were up against seemingly impossible odds at many points. Though we simply wanted to divorce amicably with limited court involvement, we were in constant battles for years. Now we choose to look at our stories as a passage to this place from which we can give back. What we have endured will make us more trustworthy guides, and provide more clear understanding, as we travel through the best half of our lives.

References

1. Blush GJ, Ross KL: Sexual allegations in divorce: the SAID syndrome. Conciliation Courts Review 1987; 25:1:1-11
2. Ross KL, Blush GJ: Sexual abuse validity discriminators in the divorced or divorcing family. Issues in Child Abuse Accusations 1990; 2:1:1-6
3. Blush GJ, Ross KL: Investigation and case management issues and strategies. Issues in Child Abuse Accusations 1990; 2:3:152-160
4. Wakefield H, Underwager R: Personality characteristics of parents making false accusations of sexual abuse in custody disputes. Issues in Child Abuse Accusations 1990; 2:3:121-136
5. Rand DC: The spectrum of parental alienation syndrome (part I). *Am J Forensic Psychology* 1997; 15:3:23-51
6. Rand DC: The spectrum of parental alienation syndrome (part II). *Am J Forensic Psychology* 1997; 15:4:39-92
7. Follingstad, DR. A measure of severe psychological abuse normed on a nationally representative sample

of adults. J Interpers Violence. 2011 Apr;26(6):1194-214. doi: 10.1177/0886260510368157. Epub 2010 Jun 28.
8. Baker AJL. *Surviving Parent Alienation: A Journey of Hope and Healing. Lanham Maryland*: Rowman and Littlefield; 2014.
9. Clawar SS, Rivlin BV: Children Held Hostage: Dealing with Programmed and Brainwashed Children. Chicago, American Bar Association, 1991
10. Johnston JR, Campbell LE: Impasses of Divorce: The Dynamics and Resolution of Family Conflict. New York, The Free Press, 1988
11. Gardner R: Recent trends in divorce and custody litigation. Academy Forum 1985; 29:2:3-7
12. Wallerstein JS, Kelly JB: Surviving the breakup: how children and parents cope with divorce. New York, Basic Books, 1980
13. Jacobs JW: Euripides' Medea: a psychodynamic model of severe divorce pathology. American Journal of Psychotherapy 1988; XLII:2:308-319
14. Reich W: Character Analysis. New York, WR Farrar, Straus and Giroux / Noonday Press, 1949
15. Wallerstein JS, Blakeslee S: Second Chances. New York, Ticknor & Fields, 1989
16. Turkat ID: Divorce related malicious mother syndrome. Journal of Family Violence 1995; 10:3:253-264
17. Thoennes N, Tjaden PG: The extent, nature, and validity of sexual abuse allegations in custody visitation disputes. Child Abuse & Neglect 1990; 12:151-63
18. Merriam-Webster. Folie a Deux, 2019. https://libguides.library.arizona.edu/c.php?g=122857&p=802721. Accessed 8/25/2019.
19. Wakefield H, Underwager R: Personality characteristics of parents making false accusations of sexual abuse in custody disputes. Issues in Child Abuse Accusations 1990; 2:3:121-136
20. Rogers M: Delusional disorder and the evolution of mistaken sexual allegations in child custody cases.

References

American Journal of Forensic Psychology 1992; 10:1:47-69

21. Baker AJL, Fine PR. Surviving parent alienation: A journey of hope and healing. Rowman & Littlefield Publishers (April 4, 2014).
22. Bone JM, Walsh MR. Parental alienation syndrome: How to detect it and what to do about it. *Florida Bar Journal*, 1999: *73*(3), pp.44-48.
23. Childress C, Attachment based parental alienation (AB-PA): A scientifically based model of parent alienation. https://drcraigchilressblog.com/2015/04/03/coping-with-the-trauma-of-parent-alienation/. Accessed 8/3/2018.
24. American Psychiatric Association's Diagnostic and Statistical Manual of Mental Disorders, fifth edition (DSM-V). 2012. Viewed 2/2/17 at http://www.psi.uba.ar/academica/carrerasdegrado/psicologia/sitios_catedras/practicas_profesionales/820_clinica_tr_personalidad_psicosis/material/dsm.pdf.
25. Stout M. The sociopath next door: the ruthless versus the rest of us. *Three River Press*, 2005.
26. Dependapotamus. https://www.urbandictionary.com/define.php?term=Dependapotamus, 2013. Accessed 8/3/2018.
27. Joiner TE. Why people die by suicide. Harvard University Press, 2015.
28. Joiner, T. E., Jr., Van Orden, K. A., Witte, T. K., Selby, E. A., Ribeiro, J. D., Lewis, R., & Rudd, M. D. (2009). Main predictions of the interpersonal–psychological theory of suicidal behavior: Empirical tests in two samples of young adults. *Journal of Abnormal Psychology, 118*(3), 634-646.
29. Florida State University, Practice makes deadly perfection, FSU suicide researcher says. https://www.fsu.edu/news/2006/01/11/deadly.perfection/. Accessed on 6/12/2019.

References

30. O'Donnell J, Logan J, Bossarte R. Ten-year trend and correlates of reported posttraumatic stress disorder among young male veteran suicide decidents-results from the National Violent Death Reporting System, 16 U.S. States, 2005-2014.
31. Jacobs JW: Involuntary child absence syndrome: an affliction of divorcing fathers, in Divorce and Fatherhood: The Struggle for Parental Identity. Edited by Jacobs JW, Washington DC, American Psychiatric Association Press, 1986.
32. Gardner RA: *Therapeutic Interventions for Children with Parental Alienation Syndrome.* Cresskill, NJ, Creative Therapeutics, 2001

Notes

13. Normal People don't make False Allegations: That is the Lowest

1. A trigger is an event in the present that causes a person to react as if they were experiencing a past similar event. Generally, it is seen as an overreaction and confuses others because the triggering event does not warrant the current emotional response.

14. Hell Hath no Fury.....Jo turns her Vengeance Toward me

1. The following are excerpts from lengthy emails (it took over 400 hours to read and organize them); they are meant to provide evidence of Jo not being a victim but **obsessively desiring contact from Steven—repetitive and overwhelming, they bombarded Steven and disrupted his life.** During this period, Jo was also continually harassing Steven with phone calls and texts.

Acknowledgments

Thank you Karin Acree for editing this book and writing the Foreword. And Stephen Zimmer for your captivating cover and design work. Tony Acree, for inviting me into your family of prestigious authors; I am honored. Thank you Sue Black for giving me so much of your time to clarify my voice, I needed your help in this project; you have an incredible gift.

Thank you my dear husband for spending dozens of hours answering questions, being interviewed and digging up documents. I know that it was very painful at times and I recognize your sacrifices in allowing this work to come to fruition. I learned so much about you during this process and want to express my admiration for you and all that you have done. Even after all of your acts of heroism, giving the example of humility to our son is something I did not dream of asking for. You have been so open and endlessly patient with me and my spectrum of emotions working through the creation of this book. I am grateful that you appreciate how I tell our truth, and express myself, and how you don't ask me to alter the story so it's more comfortable. I am grateful to be your wife.

Lastly, to my son, my beautiful boy, I cannot be more sorry

about all that you have endured, completely innocently. Your part is the most heartbreaking. And then to offer so much interest, support and patience as I wrote this book...You are the most loving and forgiving person I know. I am grateful to be your mother.

www.ingramcontent.com/pod-product-compliance
Lightning Source LLC
Chambersburg PA
CBHW051535020426
42333CB00016B/1932